Copyright Catechism II

Practical Answers to Everyday School Dilemmas

Carol Simpson

COPYRIGHT SERIES

 LINWORTH

AN IMPRINT OF ABC-CLIO, LLC
Santa Barbara, California • Denver, Colorado • Oxford, England

Library of Congress Cataloging-in-Publication Data

Simpson, Carol, 1949–
    Copyright catechism II : practical answers to everyday
school dilemmas / Carol Simpson.
        p. cm. — (Linworth copyright series)
    Rev. ed. of: Copyright catechism. 2005.
    Includes index.
    "Companion to Copyright for schools : a practical guide, 4th ed."
    ISBN 978-1-59884-848-9 (hardcopy : alk. paper) —
    ISBN 978-1-59884-849-6 (ebook)
    1. Copyright—United States.   2. Copyright—United States—
Miscellanea.   3. Fair use (Copyright)—United States.   4. Fair use
(Copyright)—United States—Miscellanea.   I. Simpson, Carol, 1949—
Copyright catechism.   II. Simpson, Carol, 1949—Copyright for schools.
4th ed.   III. Title.

KF2995.S56   2011
346.7304'82—dc23   2011022540

ISBN: 978-1-59884-848-9
EISBN: 978-1-59884-849-6

15   14   13   12   11   1   2   3   4   5

This book is also available on the World Wide Web as an eBook.
Visit www.abc-clio.com for details.

Linworth
An Imprint of ABC-CLIO, LLC

ABC-CLIO, LLC
130 Cremona Drive, P.O. Box 1911
Santa Barbara, California 93116-1911

This book is printed on acid-free paper ∞

Manufactured in the United States of America

NOTE: The information in this book should not be relied upon as legal advice. For legal questions, please consult your organization's legal counsel.

Contents

About the Author

C arol Simpson, JD, EdD, is a retired associate professor in the College of Information of the University of North Texas and practices school law. She is the author of several Linworth books on copyright including *Copyright for Schools: A Practical Guide, Fifth Edition* (Linworth Publishing, 2010).

Introduction

This book is intended as a companion to *Copyright for Schools: A Practical Guide, Fifth Edition*. While not containing the detail to be a primary resource on copyright, this book includes 178 questions taken from *Library Media Connection* (2005–2011), plus new questions not yet published. All questions have been updated to reflect the state of law as of Spring 2011. All questions were initially submitted by educators and edited for broadest application.

The most common use for the questions here is to present practical applications of copyright practice to educators who may not know or accept it. In fact, the questions and answers may be used to convince reluctant educators that their erroneous assumptions about common educational practices are incorrect. It's important to recognize that these questions are not legal advice. While the author is an attorney, I recommend that complex copyright problems be discussed with a school district's retained counsel or an attorney who specializes in intellectual property. Each situation is unique, and a slightly different combination of facts may yield a totally different outcome than the examples here. Use the questions as a starting point for discussion and consideration, not as an unequivocal answer.

Remember as you read the questions that it is essential to assert all available fair use rights, lest they be deemed to be extraneous. Free use of limited amounts of copyright-protected materials for the purpose of educating students is part of copyright law. However, courts are more and more likely to find that licensing is a viable alternative to fair use. If educators hope to retain this limited right of fair use, they must be prepared to invoke the right on every available occasion, without apologies. Publishers must also be prepared to concede the small bits of material that are available for use on a limited basis. In return, educators need to follow the rules so that publishers make enough money to continue to publish the materials educators find so attractive. It's only fair.

Finally, use caution in applying rules or guidelines promulgated by groups that have not been vetted through some congressional process. Recently, some sets of guidelines and rules have come from educational groups without input from all stakeholders. Obviously, those "rules" or "best practices" are skewed in favor of educational use. Congressional processes such as CONTU (Commission on New Technological Uses of Copyrighted Works) are certain to involve all interested parties to a fair use analysis. Guidelines without such broad input should be looked upon with suspicion and should not be relied upon without the advice of counsel with specific knowledge of all relevant facts.

C. S.

Chapter One

Ownership
of Copyright

? *I have a student who has designed a logo that he wants to have embroidered on team shirts. Someone who saw his design told him that it is already in use and is copyrighted (trademarked?). How do we find out if his design is already protected by copyright? Is there a database to search, and how would you do so for a design? Does he send his design to some government office (address?) and ask to have it trademarked and let them tell him it's already used? How do I help him?*

© Trademarks must be in use in a particular industry (e.g., Apple is a trademark in both computers and in recordings), and it is the design that is specific. The point is to avoid confusion and misrepresentations. There is what is known as dilution of a trademark, which is when a design similar to one in use is used in another area.

The United States Patent and Trademark Office has the federal registrations, but most folks must hire someone to search the files. Some files are online, but this type of search will only work when there is a word or letter combination that is searchable. However, it is possible to violate the trademark of an unregistered mark, as well as a registered one (just like copyrights), so a search is advisable. When doing the search, be sure to look for similar marks (e.g., alligator and crocodile, zephyr and cipher). Those can infringe in certain circumstances. Also, you should be aware that there are also state trademarks. The rules on how to get one of those, and how to search a given state's trademark records, will vary by state.

? *Could you give me a simplified version of just what the international copyright law says? I teach in a school overseas, and I'm not sure what the rules are.*

© There is no such thing as "international" copyright law. Each country has its own laws. If the country in which you teach is a signatory to the Berne Convention, they protect the intellectual property of other countries under their own laws. You need to find out what your country's copyright law is and if they signed Berne. Then you will know where you stand.

? *If a person has written something that will be used as an internal document and wants to be sure to be credited as the creator of it, is it enough to write "copyright so-and-so 2005" on the cover? If not, what is the procedure?*

© No notice of copyright is needed, but there are other questions to ask. Was this document written as part of someone's employment (which this sounds like)? If so, the copyright in the document is owned by the employer, not the employee. Does the author intend to sue if the copyright (assuming the copyright is the author's and not the employer's) is infringed? If so, the document must be registered with the copyright office. Go to the Copyright Office website (at www.copyright.gov) for the necessary instructions. You want the instructions for a text document. Note, also, that crediting authorship is a plagiarism issue, not a copyright issue. Plagiarism is an ethical dilemma, while copyright infringement is a legal one. Authors of works created within their employment may not have a legal right to attribution.

? *A patron wrote a short story, based on actual events in her life. She is looking for places where she might submit it for publication. If someone pays her to print it, has she automatically given that organization her copyright? Can she sell it to several magazines? What if a cable channel decided to make a movie based on it after she had accepted money for a small magazine to print it?*

© Copyrights can only be transferred in writing, so just getting paid won't transfer the copyright. But she needs to read all paperwork very closely. Sometimes, endorsing the check they send you will transfer the rights to the publisher. It's safer to offer "first serial rights" to the publisher if she is seriously concerned about ownership. However, you can only sell "first serial rights" once, because once it is published, it isn't "first" anymore. If you sell the rights to the publisher (most publishers insist on that these days because of contracts with on-line database providers) and someone wants to make a movie of it, they will need to clear with the copyright owner (no longer the author once the copyright has been sold), or do their own research into the author's life. In addition, there may be a state right of publicity that must be cleared. So, they may not be able to make a movie about your life without your permission, at least while you are alive.

A publishing note: reputable publishers won't reprint something another publisher has published, at least without acknowledgement. It is unethical as an author to submit a piece to multiple magazines without informing the magazines that the piece is under consideration elsewhere.

? *A teacher friend and I have begun writing units of study based on a set of books about the world's greatest artists. We started by writing questions with answers based on information from these books. For example, the students read the book about Claude Monet and answer five or six questions that we have written in the state academic assessment format. Then we do an art project and ultimately have a big art show at the end of the year. Our principal has suggested we conduct some workshops for teachers in our school district. If this situation expands into other districts, which we think it may, we feel that it is in our best interest to start charging for the units of study that we have developed. What are the copyright regulations concerning a situation like this?*

© The problem with this plan is that you and your colleague may not own what you have created. The lessons were created for your classes, within the scope of your employment. Therefore, the units belong to the school district, not to you, unless your teaching contract says otherwise. This is a classic work-for-hire situation. That being said, simply asking state assessment-type questions that can be answered from this book series or other sources does not infringe the copyright of the book when you just mention that the book can be used to find the answers to the questions, as long as other similar sources have comparable information. The only possible concern would be that the copyright owner might feel that you have created a derivative work from the book, such as a workbook. But a few questions about facts in a nonfiction book would likely not be enough to be so closely tracked to this one work that the questions could only be answered from this one book.

? *In our student council elections, one of the candidates has requested permission to pass out a flyer with a picture of a movie character on it. The image was found on the Internet and modified (face only), then printed on about 100–300 flyers. I believe we should reject the flyer because it is 1) from the Internet, 2) a movie image/face, and 3) modified. The student's parent contends that school campaign paraphernalia is actually covered by the rules of fair use and would not be an issue of copyright infringement, either for quotable quotes or protected images. The parent claims the use is similar to how many churches can use images from the Internet for PowerPoint presentations without being in violation.*

© Every person does have a fair use right for copyright-protected materials, so one does not have to be a school student to claim fair use. However, educational fair use is a little more generous (and easier to calculate via the educational guidelines) than fair use for the average person. The PowerPoint information that the parent refers to comes from the multimedia guidelines, and those don't apply to churches anyway—the guidelines are education-specific.

However, the issue of using a famous person's image isn't one of copyright but of publicity—a state law cause of action. If you can tell who the person is, you can't use his image because it implies that the person has endorsed or authorized the use, when in fact he hasn't. The parent overstates the "school campaign paraphernalia" permissions. There is no such specific exemption in the law. And, in fact, several presidential campaigns have been sued in recent years for use of copyrighted material without permission, most notably music. However, minimal use of certain material can be used under the four-factor fair use test. You will have to go through the "weighing" test while looking at the material to determine if the four factors fall on the fair use side of the scale.

Keep in mind that there are likely trademark issues with movie characters as well as copyright ones. Trademark has its own fair use defenses, but the primary objection here will be that use of the trademarked character will cause confusion on the part of the public whether the company owning the trademark has some relationship with the candidate or somehow endorses the candidate. Companies are very protective of trademarks because if they allow them to be used indiscriminately, the marks are found to be generic (remember "cellophane" and "aspirin") and the company loses its trademark. Additionally, altering the image is an adaptation that the trademark owner may not approve.

The point that hasn't been addressed here is that this is a personal use. The school isn't distributing these flyers, the student is. As long as there is no possibility that someone might assume endorsement or approval by the school, actor, or movie company (a disclaimer, perhaps?), this is probably okay.

? *I noticed a statement on the verso of a title page, and I am not sure what it means. It reads as follows: "The moral right of the author has been asserted." Does this have a connection to copyright?*

Ⓒ Yes, moral rights are related to copyright in a way. Moral rights include the right of an author to have a work attributed to him correctly. They also include the right to prevent his work from being damaged or destroyed. Moral rights are very strong in Europe, but relatively weak in the United States, although courts are finding creative ways to enforce moral rights. There is a case in which a Monty Python bit was hacked to pieces in a "political correctness" editing. The Pythons were awarded damages under the theory that the edited work was an unauthorized derivative work. Also, the 2006 CleanFlicks case used a moral rights argument to say that if the director wanted his work "cleaned up" he would have done it himself.

? *Can you clarify somehow this "transformative" part of copyright? Is there a way to get some clear examples of what is transformative and what is an infringement?*

© Being transformative doesn't make something fair use or not all by itself. It is something that affects the first factor of a fair use analysis. In years past we analyzed "the purpose and character of the use" as only whether the use was nonprofit educational, criticism, commentary, or news reporting. Nevertheless, many recent (and not-so-recent) cases have centered *for this factor only* on whether the use was "transformative." Nonprofit educational comes in there, too, but the courts have put much more emphasis on how the work is used. In other words, putting something on the copier or on the scanner isn't transformative. You aren't creating anything *new*—you are just duplicating something someone did already. The courts seem to look more harshly at a non-transformative copy, essentially saying to school folks, "you have the Kastenmeier guidelines for what you can copy by rote." But if you take that work and turn it into something *new* and different (i.e., *transform* it), then they will look at this factor more in your favor. That doesn't mean you don't have to look at the other three factors, too, but this is how some courts are now interpreting that particular factor.

? *Our PTA group is making a T-shirt for the year. They would like to put "Got PTA?" at the bottom of it, like the "Got milk?" slogan. Would that be considered a copyright violation?*

© "Got milk?" is a slogan, and as such isn't protected by copyright. It is, however, a trademark of the California Milk Processor Board. Trademarks also have fair use claims that can be made, but those usually apply when someone is doing comparative advertising, or mentioning a product in some news sense. Basically, as long as it is apparent that you aren't associated with the trademark owner, or attempting to pass off goods as those of the trademark owner, you are fairly safe. I do know charitable organizations that used notable trademarks and received cease and desist letters for their trouble. There is some claim of a defense of parody to use of a trademark, such as making fun of the addictive nature of Coca-Cola by using the highly recognizable Coca-Cola script and colors but using the word "cocaine" rather than the "Coca-Cola" name. An acceptable parody use pokes fun at the item being used—Coca-Cola—rather than using the Coca-Cola trademark to promote or ridicule something else. Use under the parody exception must be reflexive—it must parody the item being appropriated, not used to poke at something external.

Since trademarks are easily lost through non-permitted use while copyrights are iron clad through the expiration of the statutory time limit, companies are much quicker to defend even small misuses of trademarks.

But discuss this with your attorney, and also be sure to get the attorney to look into possible actions under your state deceptive trade practices act. The consequences of those laws can vary from state to state.

? *Does the "Fair Use Doctrine" for education purposes supersede "Terms of Use?" For example, an educational website told me that copying a rubric from the site violated their terms of use to do anything but to link to the rubric on their site. I read elsewhere that Fair Use permits using other's digital images, for example, with attribution in educational works on the Web (regardless of terms of use). So does Fair Use for educational content that will be displayed over the Internet/Web supersede others' Terms of Use on the Web?*

© Fair use is the lowest common denominator of copyright. Because it is a complex assessment, most educators look first to various guidelines. Fair use has become what you fall back on when all else fails. But you can agree to a license (a license is a contract) that totally removes any fair use rights at all. This is well documented in case law on shrink-wrap and click-wrap computer software licensing. If a website has terms of use that are apparent (such as when you must sign up to use the website, and you acknowledge that you have read the terms before you may register), you are bound by the terms if you continue to use the site. Therefore, the terms of use supersede fair use, not the other way around.

? *Every year, our school hosts a school-wide patriotic speech festival. The participants choose and memorize a speech from a list of competition selections. The choices include speeches from all periods of American history. Rather than print thick packets of 40 famous speeches for each student, we would like to make them available online. That way students could simply print their chosen speech, and we will save reams of paper. Does copyright law allow the posting of speeches on our external school website? I realize that many of the speeches are in the public domain, but how about the late 20th century speeches? What is the cut-off date for public domain entry, or is that even a relevant question? Would it be advisable to post links to speeches rather than post the speeches themselves?*

© Official speeches and writings of U.S. presidents and officials are public domain by law because the presidents are employees of the U.S. government. Written speeches of private individuals are protected by copyright if the speeches were published after 1923. Some works before 1978 may have fallen into the public domain due to lack of registration or other flukes of pre-1978 copyright, so you will need to do an assessment of each of those speeches to determine copyright status before posting. A link to those copyright-protected speeches would be more appropriate than reposting the work, assuming the site where the work is posted has permission to post it. Works published before 1923 are now in the public domain in the United States, so you can use those with relative impunity.

Sharing MARC Records

? *Can we share MARC [machine-readable cataloging] re-cords? I thought that if they were purchased from a company, such as Marcive, Inc., or provided by a vendor, they may not be copied. Is this correct?*

© It will depend on your contract with that vendor. Some vendors use many records from the Library of Congress (LOC). Works of the LOC are in the public domain by law. However, if a private organization (such as OCLC [Online Computer Library Center]) created the record, it is possible they might contend to own a copyright on the record. That assertion is suspect because facts (e.g., the title transcribed from the title page) are not protectable. About the only part of the record one might be able to claim a copyright on would be the summary.

? *A class in our high school is creating an exposé type of book of their own original creative writing and artwork. These books will be distributed and advertisements sold to cover the cost. However, they have designed a cover that includes black and white copies of famous artwork and music manuscripts. There are two DaVincis, two Van Goghs, the Nutcracker Suite music, and two of Mozart's music. These black and white images will wrap around to the back and will be in color on the back. Do these famous pieces of work, because of their age, fall into the public domain, and can they be used without violating copyright?*

© The artwork should be fine. Van Gogh, the most contemporary, died in 1890. Even applying today's copyright term, the work would be in the public domain after 1960. Mozart and Tchaikovsky, if not a post-1923 arrangement, would be public domain. Tchaikovsky is the most recent composer, and he died in 1893. Remember that new arrangements get new copyrights, so always check to see that the arrangement being used is pre-1923 or the original if you want to be certain you are dealing with public domain materials.

? *We were contacted by a vendor of MARC records who explained that their MARC records were protected by a registered copyright. How can that be?*

© While the company can certainly copyright their compilation of records, the information contained within a MARC record is factual, and not likely arranged in any creative manner sufficient to receive a copyright on the records themselves. Using the public domain MARC standard, and having the same book in hand, virtually every cataloger should come up with an essentially similar MARC record. That's the whole purpose of MARC. The Copyright Office accepts most information submitted by those trying to register their works. It does not have sufficient resources to investigate the origin and validity of the claims like the Patent and Trademark Office would for a patent, for example. Also, those registering computer software don't even need to submit the entire work to the Copyright Office to receive a copyright.

Remember, at one point someone claimed a copyright on the phone book. It took the U.S. Supreme Court to hold that there was not sufficient creativity involved in compiling the phone book to make it a copyrightable work. So just because the company claims a copyright doesn't mean it would withstand court scrutiny. The vendor may be claiming a copyright in its compilation of its database of copyrighted material, however. But a given MARC record from such a database would not be independently copyrightable. Nevertheless, if you accepted a license on your use of the MARC records, you may be bound by your contract.

? *Is this practice "fair use"? In a cooking class, there is a collection of cookbooks in an office area. Each student selects and copies a recipe from a book in the office. They use their chosen recipe in preparing a meal in class. Cookbooks are not allowed into the classroom/lab area. Students copy only one recipe apiece, and they may choose from a variety of books. With repeated use by a large number of students, and over the course of a semester, a large percentage of any book might be copied.*

Ⓒ Recipes, at least recipes that are a list of ingredients and simple assembly instructions, are not protectable by copyright. The copyright that you see on the cookbook is a "compilation copyright," meaning that the selection and arrangement (and any prefatory material) are protected, not the recipes themselves. However, even without this limited copyright on recipes, this type of copying would likely be fair use because each student chooses what he copies and makes only a single copy for personal use. In that respect, this type of copying is similar to a class of students coming to the library to do research on the same topic. There is a high likelihood that many of them will make copies of similar material, but as long as they choose the copies to make and make only one copy for personal use, there should be no problem under fair use.

? *An elementary teacher had her class write a story using their favorite character from their favorite book as the main character. She wanted to use this technique so students would analyze the characterization and maintain the personality, motives, and physical traits of the character to learn about the reciprocal nature of reading and writing. Now she would like to use one of the papers as part of her National Board portfolio. Would this be fair use? Should she explain in her narrative that this work was done under fair use?*

© Teachers can certainly do this type of derivative work as a classroom activity, but I don't recommend publishing the student results, or you might be sued. Someone who used the *Gone with the Wind* characters and retold the tale from the point of view of the slaves was sued for using the characters in a commercial project, but the lawsuit was settled after a United States Court of Appeals vacated an injunction that had been granted by a district court. However, the students own the copyright in their own work, and the teacher may not appropriate that work without permission of the student or his parents (if the student is a minor).

? *During the term of her office, the former PTO [Parent-Teacher Organization] president designed a logo for use on sweatshirts, etc. Now that she is no longer an officer, she claims she owns the copyright of the logo and will not allow them to order merchandise with the logo. Since the logo was created for the PTO, does the PTO own the copyright or does the ex-president who did the work?*

© Unless the president was paid by the PTO (and therefore the work would likely be considered work for hire) or she had some contract, express or implied, that the PTO owned the work, the president does own the copyright in the work. Of course, the PTO could hire a lawyer and fight this, but that would make it a very expensive logo. Or the PTO could go ahead and use the logo and let the former president go to the expense of hiring an attorney to challenge the use. For a more economical suggestion, I'd suggest coming up with a new design.

? *A teacher created an instructional unit that she piloted with her students in the classroom, but she wrote the unit in the summer outside the school day. If the teacher sells instructional materials or an idea she created and makes money off of it, does the school district or individual school where she teaches own the instructional materials?*

© It's difficult to answer that question, even generically. Here are some things you must consider. Absent permission in the teacher's contract, any work the teacher does "within the scope of employment" belongs to the district. What is "within the scope"? Just about anything she might do, just about any time she might do it, that has to do with the subject(s) she teaches. So if a teacher teaches fourth grade science, anything related to fourth grade science that might be done to teach that subject could be construed to be the property of her district. It doesn't make any difference that she did it at home, or during the summer, or at night. Teachers typically work all those times and places for their current assignments. However, if the teacher taught fourth grade science, and she wrote a college physics textbook at home on her own time, that would NOT belong to the district.

For more information on this topic, look in standard copyright reference texts for the concept "work for hire."

Chapter Two

Print
Materials

? *I don't understand the "nine instances of multiple copying." Where are the rules listed for this? Can we only make multiple copies for students up to nine times during a semester/ year if we're copying a chapter of a book, essay, article, or short poem? What about using any of the copies again (recycling so we don't waste paper) without seeking publisher's rights?*

© The "nine instances" language is part of the Kastenmeier report created at the behest of Congress in 1976. We refer to the Kastenmeier report as the print guidelines. It is the same report where they discuss multiple copying for classroom use, and single copies for teachers. In that report the committee members put a two-page limit on copying picture books and completely prohibit copying consumable materials. Look on page 7 of Circular 21 from the copyright office (www .copyright.gov/circs/circ21.pdf). When you make multiple copies for students, the guidelines tell you that the copies must go to the students because they specifically say you can't "accumulate" the copies, and you can't copy the same item again in a subsequent term. So, yes, if you need the same material copied semester after semester (for one-semester classes) or year after year (for full-year classes), you need to purchase the rights or get permission.

? *If we have a textbook for each student, am I allowed to copy a page out of the book and distribute it to the students so they can write on it?*

© If this is a one-time event, that use is probably fair. If this is repeated every term with the same item, however, then there is a fair use issue. The print guidelines aren't favorable to repeated copying of the same item without permission. Falling back on the four-factor fair use assessment, the use is for non-profit educational purposes, and the copy is one page out of a much larger work. Your copying probably has no impact on the value of or market for the work, unless you are making multiple instances of copying from this work, in which case the total volume may begin to substitute for purchase of the work. I don't know if the material you wish to copy is creative or factual, so you will have to decide how that factor will fall.

? *An academic team would like to make several copies of numerous pages from books that state "no portion of this book may be reproduced or copied without written permission of…" Is this "fair use?"*

© A notice in a book cannot override federal law regarding fair use. However, a signed contract or license (and in some areas of the country a shrink-wrap license) can. It is impossible to answer the question without knowing the book, where it came from, how it was acquired, etc. Copying for classroom use, in limited amounts as suggested in the print guidelines, is permissible. Going far beyond that limit is probably NOT fair use. This appears to be, from the description in your question, an extracurricular use. In that case, all of the classroom guidelines go out the window and you fall back on standard fair use—the four tests. You have to consider if this work is creative, if it is published, whether the use transforms the original work, if the use is non-profit, how much of the work you are using, and what effect the use will have on the market for or value of the work. However, if you have licensed these materials, and the license says they can't be copied, all bets are off. The license controls.

? *One of our library technicians made a PowerPoint by scanning all of the pictures in a book. She shows the PowerPoint as she reads the book. She is using it the way we more mature folks used to use an opaque projector, when we put the whole book under the lens so that everyone could see it. Because she is scanning the entire book, is this an abuse of copyright? Or is it okay since she is giving proper attribution to the author and the illustrator because she is introducing, reading, and then discussing the book itself, and just using the PowerPoint presentation to enrich the lesson?*

© Copyright wise, she is copying the entire work. There are very few "fair uses" that would allow making a copy of an entire work, and most of those involve imminent destruction of the original. Per the multimedia guidelines, she can copy about five images from a book, but I doubt that would cover a picture book. I'd recommend using a document camera instead. You are projecting the item, but the display is ephemeral—it isn't saved and stored. Showing a book during storytime is a protected use for libraries. No worries there. It is the copying and saving that is the problem.

? *Our drama teacher wants to use a script from an online site for her classes. The production will later become a public performance at the school. This site has scripts that are rewrites of popular movies, but the site does not indicate that any permission has been granted from the producers. The school principal is questioning the teacher's use of these scripts for her classroom and performance.*

© Using this script for public performance is just a disaster looking for a place to happen, especially if you advertise it. The use of a movie script in class would probably be fair use except that you have reason to believe that this copy could be infringing. Fair use is always predicated on a legal copy. And the reason the teacher is using these scripts rather than purchasing commercial copies is to deprive the producer of a sale. If you have a board policy requiring copyright compliance, that is probably the basis for your principal's (commendable) concern.

All that being said, remember that ideas cannot be protected by copyright. So anyone could write a movie script about an intergalactic war, or about a professor who travels all over the world having adventures while searching for ancient artifacts. Of course, even those scripts would be protected by a copyright owned by the screenwriter, so make certain you have performance rights with anything you plan to perform.

? *One of our teachers would like to make an audio copy of individual chapters in her social studies textbook for several students who have extremely low reading ability. She would like to download it onto the laptops of the students who need it. I'm not sure if they qualify for special education or not. Is this permissible? Would she be able to keep this recording indefinitely? What would the teacher have to do to help these students who cannot read the textbook? It's becoming increasingly frustrating to have the technology to do these kinds of things for students, yet not be able to help them.*

© No, this use is not permissible under fair use. She has the ability to make a copy of *one* chapter but not multiple chapters. There is a special exception for students who are unable to use standard print, but it isn't clear that all these students qualify for that exception. In addition, the exception specifies that the format must be in the "Recording for the Blind" or other specialized format that isn't playable on standard cassette players. There is no specific provision for computer playback, though any standardized screen reader that doesn't save a copy of the work should be an ephemeral (and thus an arguably fair) use. I understand your frustration, but the law hasn't caught up to the technology yet. Your options right now are to request permission from the publisher (who is very likely to give it since you did buy the books) or contact your congressman and hope for a change in the law (which is very unlikely considering the pro-business stance that Congress has adopted). For any students who do qualify for the "unable to use standard print" exemption, you should assist them in registering for services from your state library, the Library of Congress Division of Blind and Physically Handicapped, or the National Instructional Materials Access Center.

? *A teacher wants to type a couple of pages out of a textbook and leave important words out, putting blanks instead. She wants the students to read the textbook and fill in the blanks on the page she's typed up. (I think this is mainly so she'll know they read the pages.) It would be less than 10 percent of the work, but she's changing the format.*

© This use is easily fair, but it can't be repeated from term to term with the same work without permission, just as with any copying situation. One time only under fair use. My concern would be if she plans to do that repeatedly from the text throughout the year, or is this a one-time thing? If this is a teaching technique she plans to employ, she might want to discuss it with the textbook publisher. They may have some arrangement with your state or district for adopted texts that will allow such uses.

? *I want to create a podcast for my read-aloud times so that when a student is absent they can listen to the podcast and stay current with the read-aloud. If this plan is in violation of copyright, would there be a certain percentage of the book I could read for the podcast, and would there be a time limit it could stay available?*

ⓒ Making a podcast of an entire book is the same as making a photocopy of an entire book. An audio recording is a "phonorecord" and is covered exactly the same as any other type of copy. There isn't any educational fair use guideline that will permit making a copy of an entire work, and the general fair use guidelines generally won't support a complete copy of anything absent some obsolete format or damage to the original under certain circumstances.

Since you are reading picture books at storytimes, if you extrapolate from the print guidelines, you can copy no more than two pages of a picture book as long as those two pages don't exceed 10 percent of the text of the book. The other issue that comes up with podcasts is distribution. How will you get the podcast to the student? Making it available generally on the Internet is distribution to the world. There isn't going to be much of a fair use defense for distribution that broad. Under the TEACH Act [Technology, Education, and Copyright Harmonization Act], it may be possible to make a recording that would be available to students enrolled in a specific class, but this doesn't really meet that requirement. TEACH is a complex set of requirements, all of which must be met before you qualify for the exemptions to mount materials on the Web.

? *My teachers wish to use previous, released high stakes tests, but they do not want to give the tests in their entirety because some of the questions are on material that has not yet been covered. Rather than give the entire test, they want to pull (for example) all of the chemistry questions to use when they teach chemistry. The copyright information from the state education agency website states that "Any portion reproduced must be reproduced in its entirety and remain unedited, unaltered and unchanged in any way." They do not plan to change the questions but would like to choose which questions to use.*

© My question back to you would be, "What does 'portion' mean?" Does it mean an entire test, a section, or a question? Vocabulary is very important in interpreting licenses (which is what permission is), so it is critical to find out what that term means. You would be well served to ask the state agency.

? *If we buy a workbook that is supposed to be a consumable, may we reuse it each year? We have enough for each student to have one. May I copy pages of these to distribute to students? May I continue to copy these in future years without distributing the books to the students? I'll keep them on the shelf so that the students don't damage them.*

© You can reuse the workbooks, yes, but you cannot "reuse" them by making copies. There is a specific prohibition on copying ANY consumable. You could keep the workbooks, have students write the answers on their own paper, and use the books again each year, but you will have a difficult time doing that without letting the students touch the workbooks. Of course, all bets are off if you can get permission from the workbook publisher to allow you to reproduce the workbooks.

? *More than ever, principals wish to place materials purchased for teachers in the library circulation system. When titles say, "reproduction … for an entire school or school system is strictly prohibited," I have been advising against placing those materials in our circ system. However, a principal who purchased a book for each teacher on the grade level wants to place all five titles in the circ system and check them out to the five teachers. Any advice?*

© Putting the material in the circ system is a far cry from reproduction for an entire school. What the books are prohibiting is making photocopies of materials from those books in a systematic manner: for everyone in a given grade level from a single copy of the book, for example. As long as an individual teacher decides to make copies, and the copies comply with all the other quantity and quality requirements of the print guidelines, teachers can even make copies from these materials, for their own classes. The principals are wise to check out those materials to the teachers to maintain accountability—otherwise the teachers will leave and take the materials with them. By putting the materials in the circulation system, they are tracked and accounted for.

? *We have some copies of old textbooks that we've stopped using. May I continue to use the supplementary resources (copy worksheets, text pages, etc.) from these?*

© Are any of these materials consumables? Remember that there is a prohibition on copying consumables. You can certainly let students read the books or do exercises on their own paper, etc. Material from textbooks could be used following the standard print guidelines. There is no additional consideration given to former textbooks.

? *We have a student with severe cerebral palsy. He can read print but is eligible for services from the Library of Congress Division of Blind and Physically Handicapped because he cannot hold a book or turn a page. We would like the student to be able to read print independently (not just listen to an audio book); now he can only read a print book if someone holds the book and turns the pages for him. If we scan each page of a book and put it into a PowerPoint presentation, the student could then read the print on screen and go to the next page by using a head switch. Is this a copyright violation, since a PowerPoint presentation is not a specialized digital format? The teacher is looking for something the student can use independently at home that is not so cost prohibitive as a Kurzweil machine for home use.*

© The allowances for fair use for patrons unable to use standard print are relatively recent. However, the law does specify that the formats for those materials be limited to those "formats exclusively for use by blind or other persons with disabilities" (Section 121). In fact, the law goes on to say that copyrighted material "shall (A) not be reproduced or distributed in a format other than a specialized format exclusively for use by blind or other persons with disabilities." When you see "shall" in a law, that means there are no exceptions unless listed elsewhere in the law. Your school could use something like a Kurzweil machine or Jbliss imaging system, or avoid the copyright problem by using something like the FLIP page turner from Ablenetinc.com. You might also try going to the National Instructional Materials Access Center, specified in the law as a repository of digital materials for handicapped students placed there by the publishers for distribution to students and schools. There is a chance they might have (or could get) the material you desire. Of course, you can always ask the publisher of the material for permission for use beyond that allowed in section 121.

? *A teacher wants to download an online version of Chaucer's The Canterbury Tales. He wants to take less than 10 percent of it and translate it, then distribute it to his high school students. His reasoning is that he has not found a very good translation of the original text, so he wants to take a sample of a downloadable version and compare it to a copy that he has reason to believe is a more accurate translation. Because it is in electronic format, it would be easier to change it. The question is, can a teacher take a downloadable format of a classical piece of literature, take less than 10 percent of it, and change its format? Is this copyright violation considering that this story is centuries old?*

© Is the online version an accurate version of the original Middle English? The Middle English version is public domain and he can do with as he sees fit—reproduce, adapt, whatever. Any modern adaptations may or may not be protected by copyright depending on a number of factors, including when published, registration, renewal, etc. You would have to research the particular version to determine if it is protected. If the version is protected, he can follow the print guidelines for how much he can reproduce *one time* without permission. So that would mean he could reproduce a protected version in its original format now, for this term, but if he wants to use it again, or if he is going to use it six-plus weeks or so from now, he needs permission. If he requests permission and hears nothing before the date of needed use, he may use it *one time* without permission.

Remember that the print guidelines only apply to reproduction. If you are doing a translation, you are making a derivative work. If the source from which the teacher is working is not the true original (Middle English) version (or another version that has lapsed into the public domain), someone has already created an adaptation that you are further adapting. You must rely on the standard four-factor fair use assessment to evaluate if your proposed adaptation is fair. The facts as you present them seem to be on the fair side of the scale, but remember that just a small change in the facts can yield a totally opposite result.

? *I have used prepared reader's theater scripts with my students. I want to use these more as one of my goals this year in order to build fluency. In addition, my teachers who have responsibility for the gifted students want their students to write their own scripts. Can you tell me the legality of writing scripts and even copying prepared scripts written by others and obtained legally?*

© Writing scripts? Writing your own scripts shouldn't be a problem, if they are used within your classroom. It's when you adapt someone else's story for reader's theater and start doing public performances or selling the scripts that you would likely face copyright issues. Making copies will fall under the standard print guidelines just like other types of copying.

? *Several reading workshops suggest blowing up very short stories or news articles and posting them on a "Reading Wall" in the halls at school to generate more interest in reading. I am concerned about changing the size.*

© According to the congressional guidelines on educational uses of print materials adopted just after the last major copyright revision in 1976 (which stand unchanged today regarding print materials), a teacher may make a single copy of a chapter, short story, essay, poem, and the like and retain that copy for use in teaching. A Reading Wall within (or just outside of) the classroom would likely meet that requirement. There is nothing in the guidelines that says the allowed copy must be a photocopy. The guidelines were written long before photocopiers were commonplace, so they anticipated hand copying, among other methods of reproduction. Putting the single copy as a poster, or on a transparency, would probably be a reasonable interpretation of that guideline.

? *One of my teachers wants to make copies of the lyrics of "We Can Work It Out" by the Beatles for her students to look at as they listen to it. They are studying* The Outsiders, *and she then wants her students to use the lyrics as a reflective activity and relate them to the theme of* The Outsiders. *Is she within Fair Use guidelines?*

© Under the print guidelines, she can make a transparency or poster of the lyrics and use that for as many years as she wishes. Song lyrics are like poetry in that respect. If she makes print copies for every student in the class, she must follow the print guidelines for length. (Is it longer than 250 words? If so, she can only copy 250 words, she can make the copies only *one time*, and the copies must belong to the students and may not be retained by the teacher for future years.) Any subsequent use will require permission. She has to make this decision so close to the use that she can't get permission. (She needs no permission if her use will be in the next two weeks, for example, but if using the copies months from now, the rules certainly imply an attempt to get permission.) She can't charge for the copies. She can't make extra copies "just in case someone loses his copy." She can put the lyrics in a PowerPoint presentation, but she must follow the lyrics length limits imposed in the multimedia guidelines, unless she can justify more under a four-factor fair use assessment.

? *In creating an anthology of poetry for our different grade levels to use in writing, one teacher suggested that we collect different complete poems from different poetry collections, retype them, and reprint them within our district. Is it okay to do this if each poem is no more than one-twelfth of the collection it came from? We think this should be okay because of fair use. Or is each poem a complete work? In that event we don't think it matters what the ratio is because it is like taking just one song from a record/CD/etc. This is a violation of copyright regardless of fair use.*

© The copyright guidelines (a.k.a. the print guidelines, since print was really all there was back in 1976 when they were facilitated and endorsed by Congress) are quite specific that you are not able to make an "anthology" if doing so takes the place of textbooks or purchased reprints. That is part of the "cumulative effect" test. Your use seems to fall into that prohibited area. Also, under those guidelines each class only has nine instances of "free" multiple copying per course, so if you planned to use more than nine poems you would be over that allowance anyway.

? *A class has a textbook for each student, but the teacher wants to copy some of the pages for the students. One reason is the books are harder to give out than the copied pages and harder for the students to work with. Another reason is she wants the students to be able to write on the pages and doesn't want them to write in the books. Is it okay for her to copy some of the pages since we have a copy of the book for each student? I know we're not supposed to make copies to keep from purchasing books, but we have a copy for each student, so that excuse would not apply.*

© Some multiple copying for educational purposes is certainly fair use, but you are correct that if you are copying to avoid purchasing books your copying is probably not fair. To assess if you are exceeding what would be considered "fair," figure out how much you are copying. Start looking at the print guidelines to see where you may cross over the line. Typically, the guidelines for educational uses allow one chapter from a book. Depending on what your teacher is planning to copy, she may exceed that guideline. Of course, guidelines are guidelines, and a slight variation is probably not fatal. Nevertheless, you will have to make the assessment based on what she actually plans to copy. And of course, since you did purchase the books, the publisher might just give you permission to make the copies you would like to make. It's certainly worth a phone call or email.

? *We have 60 copies of a small book that a grade level needs to use. Unfortunately, we have over 100 students in that grade level, and each student needs a book. We have ordered 40-plus more from Amazon.com, but they have not come in yet. The teacher wants to photocopy the first two chapters plus introduction for the 40-plus students without books so that she can get started on the unit tomorrow. Those pages (17) are more than 10 percent of the total work (150 pages). The closest I come to any similar example is under music, when the teacher may copy pieces if the performance time is here, but the purchased copies have not yet arrived. Any help/advice you can send our way would be most helpful. I have looked at the publisher's site, but they do not give permission by phone or email, and written permission takes three to five weeks. Can the teacher make the copies?*

© As a general rule, when you have sufficient copies of books on order, you can copy—one chapter at a time—material that you need in class until the ordered books arrive. But don't start copying until the purchase order goes out. Just sending the order to the central office isn't sufficient. Remember that the print guidelines say that copying shall not "substitute for the purchase of books ..." Since you have ordered the books, your copies are not substituting for anything. Make sure that the school does not keep the copies it makes of the chapters. Copies made for students under fair use must belong to the students.

? *There is a man who is doing a history of sports in our district. He wants to use school annuals and scan pictures, etc. Some of these annuals go back to the '20s. What are the copyright issues?*

© Anything published in the United States before 1923 is in the public domain. But you have a host of other issues to consider as well.

The photos may be copyrighted by the photographers. Prior to 1978, anything protected by copyright had to be registered and have a copyright notice on it. The originals of those photos could be copyrighted or not—we don't know if we can't see them. Certainly, any photos are automatically copyright protected after 1989 and needed no registration or copyright notice to be protected.

Another issue is the right of publicity. An individual has a right of publicity in his/her own image. If the image is recognizable, and the individual doesn't wish to be associated with the school (maybe that person was expelled, rejected as prom queen, who knows?), he or she might, and could, object. That is a state law cause of action, not copyright. Whether the right of publicity is something you should worry about will depend on what state you are in. In California, for example, the right of publicity continues after the death of the person. In other states, however, the right dies with the individual. Consult your district's legal counsel to know the rules where you live.

? *My middle school is creating a website as part of the reporting requirement of a literacy grant we have received. We would like to include a page where parents, students, and community members may review a list of books and make recommendations on which ones to consider for purchase. As part of this page, we would like to create links to a page of summaries/reviews. Is it permissible to copy these summaries/reviews from sources such as Amazon or the publisher's websites, and if so, must we obtain permission to use them? In the case of a review on Amazon, would we have to go back to the journal for permission? In addition, is it permissible to use an image of the book cover beside each summary?*

© You will need permission for the book covers (those are owned by the publishing company) unless you have a subscription to something like Syndetic Solutions (www.syndetics.com), which licenses rights to the images. As for the user-contributed reviews on Amazon, those are either the property of Amazon (if giving ownership of the review is a condition of posting one) or the individual author. From personal experience, the posted review of my copyright book on Amazon was for another author's book, so I wouldn't trust that site for reliable information. Just because something is on the Web doesn't mean it isn't protected by copyright. The same permissions apply as if you were going to reprint something in its entirety from a public newspaper. You aren't doing commentary on the review; you are just republishing it. There is no good fair use argument here when you are using ALL of something, aren't making any transformative use, and are distributing it to the world. As an alternative suggestion, why not just *link* to the online reviews rather than republish them. Linking is generally a fair use, whereas copying is not nearly as clear.

Chapter Three

Graphic
Materials

? *In our Communication Graphics class, students have created calendars and other items, such as advertisements and posters, for class assignments. The emphasis is on visual attraction with few words. Each student is allowed to select the images or graphics he or she wants for the assignment. Most often these images come from the Internet. Graphics were not from royalty-free or public domain sites. The department wants to display our students' work at a Career and Technology Education exhibit at a local mall. Do you see any problems with this?*

© Students can use those graphics for personal use and education, including display within or near the classroom, with no issues. Once you remove the display to a public place like a mall, all bets are off. You can go through the traditional fair use assessment—graphic by graphic—to determine if the use of each piece meets fair use. Some of those images might also be trademarks, and trademarks have different considerations from copyright.

? *I would like to use reproductions from the Internet of book covers of the books on this year's state book award list and combine them in a collage on a "create-it-yourself" mug from Starbucks. My kids see me carry my mugs around, and I feel that this would help generate interest in the state book awards program. I would like to also make a couple of these mugs to donate to the scholarship auction for our state media conference. Would this be possible?*

© Making a copy of the images for your own personal use is fair; there are no issues with that. But when you start distributing the images, with an exchange of money involved (with publishers there to see it), you are getting on the ragged edge. I wouldn't think this would be a fair use. You are using a creative work, in its entirety, and you are reproducing it without commentary or transformation. Of course, you can always ask for permission. The publishers might agree since this promotes their material and the proceeds benefit the media association honoring their books. Don't forget to check with your state book award organizers to see if the name of the award has been trademarked. They may restrict its use for commercial purposes.

? *We had a couple of videos donated to us, but they were missing cover art. Would it be fair use, or a copyright violation, to use an image of the original cover in its place?*

© You can always copy to repair damage to a legitimate copy (you have something akin to a missing "page"), so there should be no problem replacing the missing cover art. Just make sure that the video copies you have are legitimate and are not copies themselves.

? *Each year, my desktop publishing class produces a student directory as a major project, with a different theme every year. This year, my staff would like to use superheroes as the theme, with four different groups of cartoon superheroes to represent the four classes in our high school.*

The educational use part of the law seems to apply to us, but in order not to have to produce nearly 400 directories (which would take the entire year), we charge a nominal fee (four to five dollars) for the directories to cover our outside printing costs. All proceeds go directly back to our desktop publishing "account" in our school's bank account.

Does this violate the "commercial gain" part of the copyright use agreement? If it does, do you know if it is feasible to get permission from the various copyright owners?

© Doing this project in class, for class experience only, is a fair use. You need no permission for that. However, you suddenly become commercial once you start selling the directory, and you lose the educational exemptions for that portion of your project. You still have standard fair use options, however.

You reference a "copyright use agreement." I'm not sure what this refers to. If you have clip art that you are using, you are bound by whatever license is on that clipart. If you are finding images of the superheroes on the Internet, scanning from books, etc., or even just using their names, you have more than copyright to worry about. All those names and images are trademarked as well as protected by copyright. Trademarks are marks that have no expiration date as long as they are being actively used in commerce. In order to protect the trademarks, the owners must protect the marks from unauthorized use that might in any way imply endorsement or association. While there is fair use for some trademarks (in product comparisons, for example), this use probably doesn't qualify for those defenses.

You will likely need permission. The way to get permission is to do a little research on who owns the copyright/trademark on those characters. It may be the comic syndicate, or it may be the illustrator/author. In any event, that is the person/company you need to approach. If the owner is a company, email or U.S. mail is appropriate (you want the request and the permission in writing), and you should send your request to the attention of the permissions department or the legal department. Sometimes the character's Web page will have appropriate links for permission requests. Describe as fully as possible how you will use the image or name and what benefit the school will receive. You may be able to negotiate a low payment that you can roll into your costs for the directories.

? *Our art teacher wants to use famous artwork in a book she is writing. The book will be a teaching guide to show famous artwork that people may not recognize in a commercial or in a coloring book. One example is a SpongeBob calendar, and each page is SpongeBob in a famous painting such as Grant Wood's* American Gothic. *Another example is a takeoff of Norman Rockwell's self-portrait with three pictures, but it features Mickey Mouse. She wonders if she will need to purchase rights to use the images or if they are in the public domain.*

Ⓒ Before she gets deep into this, she needs to investigate the images she will use. A publisher will ask these questions, so it's best she has the answers beforehand. As far as using the legacy images, those are out of copyright if the original was done before 1923. So Michelangelo, etc. are fair game. Grant Wood and Norman Rockwell, however, may not be. The other potential problem is using the SpongeBob, Mickey, etc. images. While using them in a small, low resolution format could be considered "transformative" to get a fair use claim under the *Arriba Soft* rule, the teacher probably wants to use them larger so she can point out the detail in the images. Using the images as incidental, such as icons on a timeline, would work under the *Bill Graham Archives* ruling, but she is going to be using the images as a central focus. The fact that she is using them for criticism and commentary is good, but not dispositive of all four fair use factors. The works are creative, and she is using all of them, so that puts her down 50 percent. The lynchpin will be the fourth factor—how the proposed use impacts the market for or value of the works. Because she is making money on the use of the images, some of the publishers will object. Others won't mind. Whether your friend will be able to get that book published will depend on how risk averse the publisher is. Many publishers will insist on permission from the copyright owners of images used in a book.

Public Display | *Comic Superheroes*

? *Our student council plans to use famous comic book characters in this year's "Teachers Are Superheroes" theme. They will create posters with these characters and display them around the building. Does this fall under "fair use"?*

© Students using (copying) works of art (including cartoons) for their personal use to become better artists (or just for fun) is fair as long as the copies remain with the student and the work is kept private. Your situation does not involve direct teaching, so you have lost the educational exemption there. However, as with all uses of copyrighted materials, you can do a standard fair use assessment on the situation:

- The nonprofit use is good, but this isn't criticism, commentary, or news reporting. It isn't educational, either. (*Educational* is best explained by substituting the idea of direct teaching.)

- The work is creative, but it is published, so that factor is a split. (Creative works are controlled more strictly; published works are more freely usable than unpublished ones.)

- I don't know how much of the work you are using, so I can't decide this factor. You may be doing an adaptation of the superhero graphic, which could be even iffier.

- You are making the copy to avoid paying for clip art or other licensed art, which is not good. (Such use impacts the market for the work or licensing of the work. Any time you take money out of someone's pocket, this factor does not generally fall in your favor.) Of course, if there are no commercially available images for you to use, this factor may be less important.

In addition, the superhero characters are trademarked, and trademarks are highly protected. I would recommend the students contact the comic syndicate or the publisher—whoever owns the copyright. I know that many of the comic book publishers are almost as litigious as Disney, so contacting them is a good plan. As an alternative, you can have an artistic student draw some type of original superhero and use that with just a slight adjustment in the campaign.

? *Can I scan book covers and post them to my website with student reviews? The LM_Net archives illuminate the conflicting points of view regarding this issue. My instructor for my Web Design class said he thought it was within fair use guidelines. What's your opinion?*

© You have the fair use right to make a copy of one graphic from a book and retain that graphic for use in teaching. However, redistributing that graphic to the world is *not* a fair use right. There are companies (Syndetic Solutions, for example) that sell rights to book covers in electronic format for such uses. Remember that taking money out of someone's pocket fares poorly in a fair use analysis. If there is licensing available, courts have started to consider that option as weighing against a finding of fair use on the fourth factor of a fair use assessment. Here, this use is far from a private use (on the Web is distribution to the world), and there is licensing available. Some publishers may not care; others do. But you don't get to make that decision. Some may argue that the use is transformative in that the reviews are criticism or commentary; but the review isn't of the book cover, it is of the content of the book. It's a judgment call here. Now that publishers can make a little money from the book cover images, they may be less likely to turn the other cheek regarding use. Depending on how risk averse you are, you may just want to license the images.

? *Our chorus teacher plans on showing a PowerPoint of patriotic images while performing a song during a concert. The images come from a variety of Internet sources. This is clearly public performance, but it is in the school environment, and no more than five images from any one photographer and less than 15 percent of any one collection is all that is used. The photos are not in the public domain. First question, is she covered by fair use if she credits the photos? If the answer to that question is yes, does she need to credit each photo, or can she say something like "Photos from* National Geographic, Sports Illustrated, *etc." at the end of the slide show?*

© If the teacher is going to follow the multimedia guidelines, she has to document her uses like one would document a research paper: short citation at the point of use and full citation in a mediagraphy at the end. In addition, the multimedia guidelines require some added information on the mediagraphy (copyright owner, who may be different from the author; copyright date, which may be different than the publication date; and the copyright symbol). The guidelines also require some sort of disclaimer on the first slide that basically states that the presentation uses copyright-protected material within fair use of U.S. copyright law and that further use is prohibited.

Of course, the multimedia guidelines are designed for classroom use, but they do say that presentations may be used at workshops, etc., so you would have a good case that this is nonprofit educational use. If your chorus teacher objects to the documentation, she might look for photos in the public domain, such as those produced by the federal government.

? *Some teachers would like to have book characters painted on the walls of our school to promote reading. I feel this is in violation of copyright law but have not found "specific" information to give them.*

© This use is likely NOT fair use. The characters are not only protected by copyright, they may be trademarked. It is always a good idea to ask the artist who paints a mural to present verification of clearance of the characters. Of course, he can always paint fairy tale or folk tale characters if he creates his own rendition of them and doesn't copy the works of illustrators such as Steven Kellogg, etc.

? *I would like to add a "Book of the Month" feature to our school's website, where I give a short summary of the book, title, and author. I would like to scan a picture of the book cover and post it to go with the summary so parents and students can have a visual. Is this violating copyright law, or is it okay to do this since it is for educational purposes, and I give credit by posting both author and publisher?*

© Just giving credit isn't really enough. Moreover, the author of the book probably didn't do that art on the cover, so crediting the book author isn't appropriate, either. If your image were only available to your students, you could claim educational purposes, but it isn't. It is available to the entire world via the Web. So here is the analysis:

- Use: nonprofit, but not educational (since it isn't for a class) and not criticism or commentary related to the image (you aren't talking about the art, in other words). It also isn't transformative (you are just copying it—there is no "value added" for the image).

- Nature: creative, but published.

- Amount: *all* of it (never a good thing).

- Effect of use on value of work: unknown since creator hasn't been consulted, but because licensing is available for book cover images, an argument that you could not purchase the image is not viable.

It is a calculated risk. Go to the publisher's website. Sometimes they have files there for download for just such purposes, and they grant permission to use them. You might be able to get the cover image from your book jobber, as well. If these methods don't work, I would request permission since your use goes beyond classroom use.

Chapter Four

Sound Recordings and Music

? *May books on CD be archived if the copy is never, ever circulated at the same time as the original? I think that if it is for a school library AND K–6 these factors make a difference.*

© The only medium that may be backed up is computer software. That would include CD-ROMS, but not audio CDs. The grade level and the fact that the library is in a school are not addressed in the law, so those factors would not come into play.

? *Have you heard of any school subscribing to music sites, such as Napster or iTunes, to download copyrighted MP3s and use for in-house video production? I can't find education-specific information on their sites.*

© While schools certainly could subscribe to those sites, I'm quite sure that the rights they get when they pay to download music don't include the necessary synch rights needed for video production. I doubt the sites have even considered educational uses of the music. Remember, those sites are only royalty collectors for the copyright owners: the sites do not own and cannot license the music for any reason other than personal use on a music device. For the types of uses you suggest, you need to contact the Harry Fox Agency. Under the multimedia guidelines, there is a 30-second limit for music in multimedia productions (including video production) when following the rest of the guidelines. A legally licensed copy of digital music could be used for those purposes.

So if you need a clip of a song and you don't own the CD, paying 99¢ to download the song from an online site is less expensive than paying $20 to purchase the CD to get a legal copy of the song to use in your multimedia production.

? *One of our teachers has purchased an audiotape of a class book, and she wants to loan the tape to a student. However, she's concerned about the tape possibly getting lost or damaged. Can she make a copy to send home with the student?*

© Making backup copies of personally owned media for use at home is fine. For example, if you purchased a tape for yourself and want to transfer the tape to your MP3 player, that is fine. However, as a school you do not have the legal ability to create archival copies of materials that are not in an obsolete format or are not damaged and unable to be replaced at a reasonable price. Media producers sometimes offer archival rights (the authority to make backup copies) with their materials or license the rights at a slight fee. You would need to contact the producer of the tape in question to see if they offer those rights for sale. Also note that there is a significant difference in what the general public is allowed to do in the privacy of their own homes (e.g., taping and retaining television programs) and what we are allowed to do in our classrooms and library media centers. It is essential that you separate those locations when calculating copyright repercussions.

? *Today I tried to order another set of* To Kill a Mockingbird *on CD or cassette and found it is out of print from all the publishers. I have looked on most of the audio vendor web-sites. If we only have one copy, is it okay to make an archive copy and circulate the copied set?*

© Is something wrong with the set? You can make a repair copy, but you can't make an "in case" copy. It works like this: you can make repair copies if "an unused replacement is unavailable at a reasonable price." In other words, if yours breaks, you can make a copy to replace it if you can't buy one at that time. But you can't start making additional copies (or archive copies) just because the work is out of print. That removes the economic incentive from publishers to republish it.

? We want to begin podcasting in our library media center but are having difficulty locating background music with the ability to podcast/broadcast. Can you suggest some sources of free or inexpensive music for this purpose?

© Broadcast rights (and podcasting is a form of broadcasting) are difficult to obtain and generally not inexpensive. However, here are three sources that may help you. The first is Free Music Archive (freemusicarchive.org). Most of the music in the Archive is covered by Creative Commons licenses, but other types of music are included, including public domain music.

A second source of podcast music is MusicAlley.com (www.musicalley.com). Works found here are available under a Creative Commons attribution license. The site even gives a short primer on how to attribute music in a podcast.

Finally, Magnatune (magnatune.com) has an amazing selection of music in virtually every genre. They do sell music, but they also offer a free "credit card" for nonprofit podcasters if you email them with the URL of your podcast. Happy podcasting!

? *We are producing podcasts right and left. At this point, it is just original digital storytelling. But when I asked an educational computing manufacturer about educational use of commercial material in podcasts, they told me that I didn't have to worry about copyright. Is that true?*

© What is being podcast? That's the primary question. There are several sites that give pretty much blanket gratis licenses for music for podcasting, but unless the podcast is direct instruction for a class, you are out of the educational fair use arena and must rely on standard fair use. If you are reading a book into a digital file for podcasting from an open website, you are: 1) making a phonorecord of the book (a complete copy, per the law) and 2) distributing it to the world from a website. None of those things are likely to make a case for fair use, even within the educational context. If you are doing the podcasting within a secure school website, the TEACH Act may come into play. You can look to its limitations if you meet all the conditions for its application.

? *Our drama teacher is making a CD with voices of our children and teachers. Her question is, how does she find out if certain popular tunes are protected by copyright? The example she gave me was "Happy Birthday" using different words. Could you tell us how we could go about finding out this sort of thing?*

© The bad news is that "Happy Birthday" is still protected for a few more years. To find out what songs are protected, you usually have to check two or three websites: ASCAP [American Society of Composers, Authors, and Publishers] (www.ascap.com), BMI [Broadcast Music, Inc.] (www.bmi.com), and SESAC (www.sesac.com). Some minor rights organizations represent specialized artists (such as certain Christian artists), but these three are the biggies.

? *I have a teacher who is making CD copies of our library audiobooks for the other special education teachers and their students. (This is so they do not have to share one audiobook.) Is this a copyright infringement? If so, what is the argument against it?*

© Yes, it is a violation. It violates the right of reproduction, a right reserved to the copyright owner. There are some *limited* educational exemptions for performance of audiobooks, but anything like this that smacks of what courts call systematic copying (buying one copy and duplicating it for multiple teachers in order to avoid purchasing legal copies) would be seriously frowned upon.

? *An online retailer is now offering audiobooks for sale on their website. They say: "Because it's digital, you can download your audio and listen right on your computer, burn it to CD, or load it up on your MP3 player, such as the Apple iPod. And don't worry about making a back-up—there will always be a copy of all purchased audio programs for you in your library to download as many times as you want." We have a special education teacher who would like to download the audiobook* Hatchet *onto an iPod that she has purchased. Can she download it onto other iPods?*

© This is a licensing issue. Unless the license states you can have multiple copies of the same program at the same time, you aren't going to be able to do that. You need to investigate very carefully the limitations on what you may do with those audio recordings. I suspect they will only allow you to have one copy at a time. And when you ask if she can load the program onto other iPods, I presume you mean iPods belonging to her students. I suspect that the license will limit downloads to the subscriber's household, otherwise one person could purchase the audiobook and distribute it to everyone she knows with no license implications. I doubt that is the intent of the license.

? *A student asked, "I want to be able to send out my next productions to festivals and competitions, but I still want music in them. The best way to do that would be to use classical/public domain songs. One that I already have in mind is "Shenandoah," the Civil War song. It plays at the end of* Nixon *and they credit it as traditional, but they also say it is courtesy of London Records. I just want to know my boundaries. Is there a way I can find out what's traditional and what's not? Or at least, what is the easiest way to do that?"*

Ⓒ Sound recordings are protected just like new works, so anything recorded after 1972 may be protected in the U.S. (assuming registration and notice for works published before 1989). The underlying composition may be in the public domain, so that is one less clearance hurdle you must get, but the recording of that public domain song still is protected by the performance copyright. The ideal thing is to use a service called Public Domain Reports. They have huge lists of public domain music and will sell you the sheet music. Then use a computer to perform the music or perform it yourself on an instrument or *a capella*. All of those are fairly foolproof ways to get PD [public domain] music. As an option, you can use some of the royalty-free discs or online services. A lot of those are downloadable by track at little expense, and you can use the songs in any way, other than re-selling the music for clips, without paying additional fees. Check the license agreement for specific limitations.

Remember, though, that student productions created under the multimedia guidelines may be retained by students and used for the student's personal use. Personal use could include competitions, but the media would have to be cleared eventually if the competition entries are mounted on the Web or performed publicly.

? *I have been trying to figure out if we can legally copy* To Kill a Mockingbird *on CD for a student who is entitled to have it according to her IEP [individualized education program]. It is not available for purchase, and we do not own a copy. It is currently out-of-print at the author's request. The audiobook can be purchased from secondary sources for usually well over $100.*

A teacher borrowed the CD from a public library over the summer and made a copy. Is she allowed to give this to the student to take home? Also, are other students allowed to borrow it even if it's not in their IEPs? Other schools in the district have this audiobook title, and it can be borrowed via interlibrary loan. We can borrow it for her, but last year there were no copies available to borrow from the public libraries in our area during the time that the student needed it.

Would I be correct to tell the teacher that, even though the recording is unavailable (out of print), it is not out of copyright and, since the audiobook is available from other sources (other schools or purchase from secondary sources), she would be in violation of the law if she copied it? I called the publishing company, and they said they didn't think copying was legal but didn't seem sure.

© Copyright law does not address IEPs. A school can put anything in an IEP, such as, "If the student has no behavioral demerits in a week the student is allowed to choose one video of his choice to watch on Friday afternoon." However, this showing does not meet the direct teach requirement of section 110 and therefore would require a public performance license. Putting something in an IEP doesn't trump other laws that may apply to the situation.

In this scenario, the teacher's copy is illegal. If you are making another copy, you will be compounding and participating in the violation. There is a provision in the law to make a *replacement* copy (meaning that you already own it, but it has become damaged, lost, or stolen), but there is no provision to make an original copy because the work is out of print. I have gotten this question on this particular title at least a dozen times recently, so there is demand there. However, if one were allowed to make original copies, the demand would go away and there would be no economic incentive for the publisher to renegotiate the rights with the copyright holder. As you are aware, copyright is an economic law, and economic motives are a significant basis for its existence. I don't see any changes in that view forthcoming.

I'm not sure why the student needs the audio copy. If he is blind or physically handicapped (unable to use standard print) or severely dyslexic (with a medical diagnosis of same), the student can qualify for the services of your state library or the Library of Congress Division of Blind and Physically Handicapped. They will certainly have this work on tape in the specialized format required for Recording for the Blind and Dyslexic. The loans are free, as are the special players required. That source would be your best and most reliable for this student.

? *A choral teacher at my school tells me that she can make a copy of any music she buys to use in her classroom as long as she has the same amount of original copies in her file. Could you clarify this for me?*

Ⓒ There is no "free copies for music" exemption, unfortunately. An individual student can make a copy of a piece of music (to annotate), but that is the student's decision. The best source for educational music copyright information is on the National Association for Music Education's website (www.menc.org). In addition, the Music Publishers Association condenses the various statutes and guidelines related to copying music (see mpa.org/copyright_resource_center/you#cancopy). What you describe would be academic purposes other than performance. If she is considering these archival copies, the only archival permission within copyright law is for computer software. You can't make a backup copy of a book, for example, on the off chance that someone would damage it. If she considers the music to be a "consumable" (like a workbook), there is a prohibition on copying anything consumable. Under the guidelines for music (www.lib.uconn.edu/copyright/guidelinesForMusic.html), you will see permission to make copies (other than for performance) of music as long as it doesn't constitute a "performable unit" not to exceed 10 percent of the work. A whole song, or complete section of a longer piece, would be a performable unit. The exemption is really intended to cover things like scales, certain difficult fingering patterns, etc. So the burden really is on the teacher to document some case law or guideline that says she has this right. I don't think she can come up with anything that supports her argument.

? *If we have a book that our students are reading that does not have an abridged audio version available, can we make an abridged version as long as we give proper credit to the original author?*

© What you are describing is called a derivative work. A lot would depend on how many copies of it you were going to make, for what purposes, and how you were going to distribute them. Remember, you are copying the "essence of the work" here, so as far as the law is concerned you are copying the whole thing. You are doing this in a way that would harm the market for an abridged copy (you aren't going to buy an abridged copy if the publisher comes out with one because you have this one), and the work is creative. However, if you are making this copy for one student, and the copy is temporary, you might be able to make a case for the temporary copy as long as it doesn't substitute for purchase of the book. You are really better off to ask the publisher for permission. If the publisher doesn't plan to market an abridged audiobook, it might give you permission, provided you aren't making digital copies. Digital is always a concern for publishers.

? *One of our school chorus groups has been asked to perform a public domain song, which may or may not be used in the soundtrack for a movie production. The recording is to take place in a recording studio, and the producer of the soundtrack has offered to record several of the choir's favorite pieces from this past year and make a CD for each of the students for their own personal use. The middle school has performance rights for the choir selections, but we are not sure if that includes the right to make CDs for each of the students in the chorus. I saw that one of your books indicated only one copy could be made for grading and evaluating purposes. Does it make a difference that the CD is being produced in a recording studio? Is it possible that the folks recording it have the right to make copies and distribute them to the students? In addition, if we had made a video or a sound recording of the performance here in the school system, could we legally make copies for the students who were part of that performance?*

© Material truly in the public domain can be recorded without consequence. However, very little music is really in the public domain. An arrangement of public domain music is protected by copyright, and you must do an analysis on the arrangement to determine if it, too, is in the public domain. So unless you can find the original sheet music and record from that, you may not be dealing with a public domain piece.

Having performance rights doesn't necessarily give you a right to record. Look on your license for "mechanical" rights. You need mechanical rights to be able to record a performance. The only exception to that is recording a single copy of a live concert, and that one copy is for the school to use only for critique of the performance.

The recording studio isn't going to have any special mechanical rights unless they expressly negotiated for them. Nightclubs and other performance venues have rights from ASCAP or BMI to do live performances of any song in the respective rights organization's catalog. But those aren't recording rights, which is why at a concert they tell you that you can't record the performance.

? *Our high school offers a television production class where students create multimedia presentations. Last week, Technology Services locked students out of their student accounts because they had MP3 files saved in them. Technology Services said that students couldn't have those files, as it is against copyright. A) If students save legally acquired MP3 files to their accounts, or a school computer, is this a violation? B) If students save legally acquired MP3 files to their accounts, and the files are backed up each night, is that a violation because Technology Services makes another copy of the file? C) Can students make a copy of an MP3 file in order to edit the file to use the appropriate length in a multimedia presentation (10 percent or 30 seconds, whichever is less)? D) Do you know of a policy that works for everyone in terms of using multimedia files in student work?*

© A) Getting MP3 files from Napster (the new Napster), iTunes, or another legitimate service is legal as long as the student has paid for (or otherwise legally acquired) the files. The problem comes when students start exchanging files with each other to avoid purchasing. If the school district is facilitating student file sharing in that way, they can become the target of the RIAA [Recording Industry Association of America] and the other copyright watchdog groups in much the same way that colleges have. B) Making a backup of your computer (including your music files) is not generally a copyright violation unless the extra copies of the files are accessible somewhere. This is no more a copyright violation than making daily backups of Word, or Windows, or any other computer software. C) They can make the clip, yes, under the guidelines. It would be impossible to use otherwise. D) I would probably recommend that kids keep their files on a flash drive so there is no problematic involvement on the part of the district, and there is no question that the files belong to the individual students.

? *The band teacher purchased the rights to a piece of music for a band concert. She has purchased one piece of music for each student/instrument. Can she make a copy of each student's music for them to keep at home and keep the original music in their band folders at school? She does not want the students to take the original music home because they might lose it or forget to bring it to school every day.*

© According to the Guidelines for Educational Uses of Music (found at the National Association for Music Education website), this is not okay. A teacher can make a copy of a portion of a work, but that portion may not be a performable unit (song, movement, etc.). Remember, copyright is an economic law, not an education law. The purpose is to accommodate schools but to hurt the pocketbook of publishers as little as possible while still achieving direct teaching. No one ever has a guarantee, when purchasing a book or piece of music, that the work won't be lost or destroyed. Fair use is not the same as an insurance policy. However, there is nothing in the law that says that a student can't decide on his own to make a copy of the work for his personal use. That copy would be okay.

? *I am interested in creating a digital yearbook on DVD in lieu of the hardcopy. We are planning to make these available for purchase by the parents. I want to use clips of music. If I follow Fair Use Guidelines and give credit, is this all I need to do? The digital yearbooks will be sold to parents.*

© You need to consult with your district's attorney on this matter, because details will be important. To help guide your discussions with that person, here are some things to remember. Any time money changes hands, there will be limitations on fair use. Digital yearbooks aren't for educational purposes as understood in the Copyright Act. Educational purposes would be for direct presentation of teaching content to students, or student use in a project in a regular class. Those who use music in the manner you describe are probably exceeding what would be considered a "fair use." I had an attorney once tell me that a music clip is too long to be considered "fair use" if you played enough of the tune to recognize what it was. A recent case involving presidential candidates' use of recorded music found that 20 seconds of a song exceeded what could be called "fair." The company that licenses synch rights (meaning music used in video) is Harry Fox Agency in New York. You can inquire about using specific pieces of music on their website.

? *I have found several radio stations that do streaming audio. If a teacher wanted background music, could he or she play this through her computer for the class?*

Ⓒ If we were talking about an ordinary radio, this would be a clearer answer. The House report that accompanied the 1976 Copyright Act explained that per section 110(5) of the act, "Secondary use of [a radio transmission] by turning on an ordinary receiver in public is so remote and minimal that no further liability should be imposed." That means that if the teacher is listening to a radio transmission, and the class happens to hear it, there should be no problem. However, a second part of that same section has been interpreted by courts to mean that there can only be one "receiving apparatus" at a geographic location. So in any school where more than one teacher has a receiver (radio or computer, as the case may be), the use may not be exempt under the act. Naturally, any direct classroom instruction using music would meet the educational exemption. A further consideration is that typically Internet services are used under some license or terms of service. You will need to check those for the Internet radio station in question.

? *Can a communications class, in which the teacher is teaching students to prepare a news program, download music from the Internet to use in student productions?*

© This appears to be face-to-face instruction. If you keep the results within the classroom, and the music you download is legally acquired (either purchased or legally downloaded), you are within a standard fair use analysis. However, if the downloaded music is protected by copyright and is downloaded from a peer-to-peer file sharing service, the copy is probably not legal and you would not be within fair use.

? *Can a band director keep an archival copy of each instrument part and give copies to students (trumpet first chair, clarinet first chair, etc.)? Student use damages originals. I see in the music guidelines that music teachers can copy up to 10 percent of a work. I assume 10 percent means 10 percent of the "parts." I thought the vendors of band music for education provided some guidelines/permissions when music is purchased for school use.*

ⓒ Making backup copies of student music is considered making archival copies of the music. There is no automatic archival right in any print material that is still protected by copyright. Only computer software may be archived, per current law. Nothing guarantees that print materials will not wear out and need to be replaced. That eventuality is considered by the publisher when pricing material.

The 10 percent that you refer to from the music guidelines means that a teacher may not copy more than 10 percent of the content of a work—meaning that you can copy a section of particularly difficult fingering, for example, for the students to use as practice material. But that 10 percent cannot constitute a "performable unit." Copying a part—such as the clarinet part—is a "performable unit" and therefore not allowed under the music guidelines.

I don't know of any blanket permission given by music publishers who sell music to schools. Similarly, there is no blanket permission given by textbook publishers or library book publishers. They are all in the business of making money by selling their materials. However, I'm sure that if a publisher would step out on a limb and, for a little extra money, grant those rights, music teachers would flock to that publisher, who would make a zillion bucks. Then perhaps others would follow suit. But just like penguins at the South Pole, the first one into the water faces some significant dangers, and everyone wants to sit back and let someone else be the pioneer.

? *We were horrified to find that we are violating copyright if we play music to our students in a classroom as a background to our activities. We've read the studies that show how music increases learning. We are wondering if we write into the lesson plan that music will be played while students are quietly working, and then quote the studies and the objectives that this would pertain to, would we be able to play the music to help our students focus their thinking without violating any copyright? Is Congress re-working this? Will we see a change in this wording anytime soon?*

© In understanding the copyright rules, you have to understand that Congress expects school to be like it was when they were in school—essentially Beaver and Miss Landers. It is their firm belief that *limited* amounts of materials may be used for *direct teaching* without paying royalties. That limited use means one time and/or a small amount. Congress believes (and they have a lot of reasoning on their side because they must support those in the economy who make a living and pay taxes from the materials they publish or create) that anything that is not direct instruction is "bells and whistles" and doesn't deserve a free ride. And no, there is no change forthcoming. In fact, I see more restrictions coming based on pressure from the music industry, which has lost more than 50 percent of its revenue to illegal file sharing. Try looking for recordings of pre-1923 classical music that were recorded before 1972. Those recordings (and the underlying compositions) are in the public domain and may be used at will.

? *Is it permissible to play a complete popular song and have it tied to a lesson, or is it still limited to 30 seconds?*

© You seem to be confusing two sets of guidelines. Remember, the various guidelines and limits are only useful for that medium. The 30 seconds for music only applies to multimedia, like PowerPoint. If you are using a song for a specific purpose in class, and playing from a legally acquired copy, you can use the entire song.

> **?** *Teachers wish to record themselves reading whole books and then push those files out to iPod Touches so students can listen. The students would then record their own voices reading the whole book and listen back, and at some point, the teacher would listen to their progress in these readings. The files would not be shared online or in any other way. The purpose, of course, is to help improve student fluency. Is this allowable under copyright?*

© There is no case law to guide this practice, so anyone's opinion is just that—an opinion. With the state of the courts these days, it's anyone's guess what a given judge or jury would decide. However, reading a book onto a recording medium of any type is exactly the same thing, copyright wise, as putting the book on the photocopier and copying every page. And she is going to do this multiple times. The publisher could make a good case that there are audio recordings of the book that could be used in place of the homemade recordings, so this is replacing an authorized copy of the work. The use isn't transformative in any way—the teacher is copying the book exactly as it was written. There is no "value added," no interpretation, no criticism or commentary. The work is creative, not factual. And she is reading it in its entirety. A homemade recording of the whole work could certainly replace a purchased recording of the work. I can't see any of the four fair use factors falling in your favor except for the educational purpose (which is only part of one factor), and that standing alone is not sufficient to support a finding of fair use. Students, on the other hand, might be able to make an excellent fair use case for the practice reading since they are making a single copy of the work for their own education, as long as the recording is ephemeral (meaning it only lasts as long as the student needs it to demonstrate his reading fluency).

? *Teachers come back from workshops in which the presenter used music throughout and recommended that participants follow suit. The music is owned by the presenter (or teacher) and is used for transitions in instruction, for example. Is this fair use for the presenter, when participants are not students and the presenter is making money from the presentation? Is this a fair use for a teacher in a classroom when it is part of the instructional process?*

© Using music for direct instruction is certainly permissible. An example of that type of instruction is a music teacher who plays a song before the students sing it, or a teacher who plays a Civil War march as an example of the culture of the Civil War era. Simply owning music does not give the purchaser public performance rights, just as owning a video does not give you public performance rights in the video, either. The fact that the presenter is being paid is not dispositive. Teachers get paid to teach school, but that doesn't disqualify their use of video if the showing meets the requirements of section 110(1). Uses of more than minimal amounts of music that are for entertainment purposes (such as transition) are not covered by fair use. Instructional use is use for a direct teach piece. Transitions are between teaching segments. It is simply "filler." There are assorted producers of royalty-free music that can be used in such situations, or the district can purchase a municipal license from ASCAP to cover all such uses of music (including only the music of the respective rights organization) for the duration and for the purposes outlined in the license. The workshop presenter may have relied on just such a license held by the venue where the workshop was held for her use of the transition music.

? *Our teacher of Music and Art Appreciation wants to take classical music CDs owned by our school and put selections in a playlist on his own iPod. He will then use this list to play for a final test, asking questions about the piece, composer, etc. Is this fair use?*

© Making copies of portions of recordings for the purpose of aural examinations is one of the permissible exemptions under the music guidelines. The guidelines say (among other things) that "a single copy of a sound recording (such as a tape, disc or cassette) of copyrighted music may be made from sound recordings owned by an educational institution or an individual teacher for the purpose of constructing aural exercises or examinations and may be retained by the educational institution or individual teacher."

? *I am training students to use a video camera, a digital camera, and video-editing software to create a daily presentation for the student body. We tape it first period and then show it to the student body at the beginning of second period. The presentation includes school announcements, booktalks, and student projects. Would we be infringing copyright if we used a few seconds of music from CDs I own? Would that be fair use? It is face-to-face instruction.*

© The first problem is that it is *not* face-to-face instruction in the legal definition of the term. Only if a teacher is presenting curricular content in direct teaching do you have face-to-face instruction. In fact, Congress had to pass the TEACH Act to get around the requirement that students and teachers had to be in the same place in order to qualify for certain educational exemptions. However the TEACH Act has its own specific requirements for exemptions.

An announcement-type program that goes to all the students in the building is not direct teaching of curricular content since not every student is studying the same things. The second problem is that "fair use" of music can be problematic if the music is recognizable. A copyright attorney recently suggested that if you can tell what the song is, you have used a "significant amount." How much is a "few seconds"? And the most problematic part of all is that you are broadcasting, which is wide-area distribution. The favorable things are that you aren't charging admission and you own the CDs. Neither is a major factor when compared to the others. I'd recommend subscribing to a clip music collection or service, or using Creative Commons licensed music for this purpose.

? *In a daily announcements program broadcast to the entire school, may we use music clips downloaded from the Internet?*

© One of the important factors in a fair use analysis is a legal copy of the work being used. But there is a lot of missing information in your question. Did you purchase the music from a site such as iTunes? Are the music and the performance in the public domain? How much are you using? All that information feeds into this analysis.

? *Can a staff development presenter play music from her computer or from a CD in the computer while waiting for the session to begin? Can the music be played while showing a PowerPoint presentation before the session begins? The music and/or CD are legal, the music has not been downloaded from an Internet file-sharing site, the music is not embedded into the PowerPoint, and the CD is the personal property of the presenter.*

© Staff development has limited fair use options. The educational exemptions disappear because this isn't an audience of students. These are employees doing job training, not students enrolled in a degree-granting institution. You have only the regular fair use tests applied to the general public. Basically, if you play enough of a song that it is recognizable, the RIAA considers it to be beyond fair use and can/will take action. You can get a license for the presentation venue to be able to play such music, however, from ASCAP and/or BMI, or the venue may already have such a license (in the case of public auditoriums, etc.). If the work is embedded into a multimedia presentation, the limit for music is 30 seconds or 10 percent of the work, whichever is less.

? *I'd like to include short excerpts from our audiobooks in previews/reviews that would be posted on our library Web page. Does that qualify for fair use?*

© A recent court case (*Brilliance Audio, Inc. v. Haights Cross Communications, Inc.*) distinguished audiobooks from musical recordings for purposes of copyright analysis in renting recordings under the Record Rental Amendment Act (17 U.S.C. § 109(b)(1)(A)). However, fair use of recordings was not discussed in the ruling. Historically, using much of any recording has not set well with courts, even under a claim of fair use, especially in light of the Digital Millennium Copyright Act's creation of a right of digital transmission of sound recordings. But there is good news! Random House (www.randomhouse.com/), among other audiobook producers, has begun granting permission to use excerpts of audiobooks as samples through library Web pages. However, you must use the excerpt that Random House provides—you cannot create your own.

? *Is an instructor allowed to make a copy of a legal public performance (play, music, etc.) and then duplicate it for each student to keep as part of his or her portfolio? I understand that students may keep a copy of their multimedia projects for such a purpose.*

© It is difficult, if not impossible, to give one answer to this question. Much will depend on what we are talking about. For example, in doing a licensed play (not something in the public domain, like original works of Shakespeare), what you can tape and what you can do with the tapes are totally controlled by the contract with the play company. In the case of copyrighted music performed by a school group, the law says there can be only one tape of the performance, and that tape must reside at the school and be used only for critique of the performance. However, if you have licensed the music, you are under total control of what terms and conditions are in the license. If you want to give a copy of the performance to each student, you should negotiate that right in the contract. Educators may be remiss in just accepting the licensing terms that the rights company proposes. Those are simply contract terms and are totally negotiable. There is no statutory requirement to limit the provisions that the company may accept.

? *Is it permissible to play a full song/CD in your classroom as background music (not tied into lessons, but simply background music, like classical)? Is it permissible to play an entire song over the morning announcements broadcasting system while we show a poster teaching the concept?*

© These aren't simple questions to answer. Depending on the classical recording, it might be in the public domain. Recordings made before 1972 were not protectable, and if they were made from music that was in the public domain (like any classical music written before about 1923), the recordings are currently in the public domain. Public domain recordings can be used for any purpose. However, playing music for background as long as you are using a typical home-type player is not a problem. Once you extend beyond a home-type player into media distribution, or the PA system, you are going to have a difficult time justifying this. At that point it becomes a nonexempt public performance, like at the mall. Remember that "enrichment" (the category that most all-school initiatives fit into) doesn't qualify for the direct teach piece that is so important for an educational performance exemption. You say you are playing the music while you are showing a poster. Is the poster about the music? Are you commenting on the music? If not, the music is just audio decoration for the poster, and your fair use claim will be much harder to make.

? *Is it permissible to play an entire song over the morning announcements broadcasting system while we show a poster teaching the concept? (e.g., we show a poster of counting by fives while playing a song that teaches it.)*

© You are going to have a difficult time with this use. There is likely no curriculum that applies to every grade in your school. Remember that "enrichment" (the category that most all-school initiatives fit into) doesn't qualify for that direct teach piece that is so important in a fair use assessment. But look at your song. It appears to be an educational recording, and it may have permissions for such uses. Failing to find any indication of the permissions granted, you might apply to the copyright owner for your one-time use.

? *A teacher is presenting at a conference, and she has created movement to go with songs. She is taking the legally purchased CD and playing it on a boom box. She is not copying anything. She is not being paid anything. If anything, she could be helping to sell the CDs. I know fair use covers classroom use and not staff development. I know for movies, this scenario would be considered public performance. What about music?*

© This is certainly public performance. The material is being performed, and the audience is greater than a family and its immediate circle of friends. But you are mistaken that there is no fair use for staff development. There is no application of the *classroom permissions* for staff development because these are employees and not students. Nevertheless, there is always fair use (the standard four-factor balancing test) available for every citizen. Possible good news: depending on where she is doing the performance, the hall may have a venue license that covers such performances. She needs to ask. Further, if she uses limited clips of music in a PowerPoint or video context, her use may fall under the workshop exemptions of the multimedia guidelines.

? *My school wants to use music instead of bells over our media retrieval system for our school passing period. I told them they could use a 30-second clip or they would have to get copyright permission to play more than a 30-second clip. Is this information correct?*

© You are confusing the 30-second limit listed in the multimedia guidelines (for PowerPoint presentations, etc.) with standard fair use. What you plan to do could exceed fair use for music (this is a public performance). I'd recommend you purchase an inexpensive, royalty-free music collection. You can use royalty-free music for this purpose with no problem. I generally recommend Soundzabound as an inexpensive source, but many other companies have similar collections. In addition, dig.ccmixter.org has many forms of Creative Commons licensed music.

? *If I am going to have students create podcasts of book excerpts for my book review wiki, how many words is considered legal?*

© I can't give you a hard and fast number of words. The Supreme Court held 300 words of a 400-plus page book to be "the essence of the work" sufficient to count for copying the whole work. Many picture books are under 200 words, total. You will need to do a fair use assessment for each work you use. Since you are criticizing the works, you will have a much stronger fair use case than if you were just reading the book.

? *Can we play the [insert university name here] spirit songs over the PA system before school starts each day?*

Ⓒ I can't say about any specific song, because I don't know when it was written. For works written before 1923, the sheet music is in the public domain in the U.S. If your school band plays that pre-1923 work, and you record it, you can play the recording on the PA. If someone else recorded a pre-1923 song before 1972, you can play the recording over the PA, because sound recordings were not protectable by copyright before 1972 and the sheet music is in the public domain. If someone else recorded a pre-1923 song *after* 1971, there is a copyright on the recording (but not on the underlying work) that you would want to clear. For songs copyrighted *after* 1923, you would need to in-vestigate the copyright status of the sheet music before you could make a determination.

? *Can popular music be played during intermission, time-outs, and such at a basketball game if there is an admission charge (not-for-profit that will be given directly back to sports)?*

© Is the music being performed by the band or students? If so, this is probably a fair use. There is a performance exemption for *sheet music* for live school performances when none of the performers are paid and any admission fees go back to the school. There is no similar exemption for recorded music (which has a separate copyright on the recording). For that, you will need a municipal performance license, either through your city (if your city government controls your school system) or through your district (if your school district is its own governmental entity).

? *I'm looking for any kind of blanket site license to play music at pep rallies, games, over the intercom, etc. We bought a movie site license and hope there might be a comparable program available for music.*

© Both ASCAP and BMI sell such licenses to public facilities, public auditoriums, stadia, coliseums, etc. They also sell them to colleges and universities. Whether you need one depends on what type of music you are playing. If students are doing the performing, none of the performers are paid, and all of any admission goes to educational purposes, you don't need a license. If you plan to play recorded music, the next question will be how your school entity is organized. If your schools are a division of the local municipal or county government, you can qualify under the local government's license with ASCAP or BMI. If your schools are free-standing governmental entities, you need to purchase a *municipal* license. Be sure to specify, when you inquire, that you are looking for a license for *non-instructional* use of music. You don't need a license for instructional use, of course, and don't want to even open the door that might imply you want a license for what would be fair use.

Chapter Five

Video
and Film

? *A teacher has some TV broadcasts recorded off-air several years ago. He has not been able to find a source from which we may purchase a copy. How do we determine that a program is no longer available for purchase? And, if it is no longer available for purchase or broadcast, is he able to use his taped version in school? Does the same rule apply as with books that are no longer available for purchase? Is it permissible to copy this broadcast in order to use it?*

© The teacher has retained these programs more than 45 days post-broadcast, so the tapes are illegal for school use (personal use at home doesn't have this restriction). This isn't the same situation ("not available at a reasonable price") as replacing a work that has been damaged. This is part of the off-air taping guidelines (still called "taping" even though few people actually use tape any more). It may be that these programs have never been available for sale, and that is the prerogative of the copyright owner. If the program is not available for sale, and the tapes are older than 45 days past the broadcast from which they were taped, your only option will be to track down the copyright owner to request permission to use the tapes. What I'm not sure of is how you will explain how you have the tapes to begin with, since under the off-air guidelines they should have been erased long ago.

? *Our senior class has a company put together a slide show set to popular music that is shown at graduation each year. The company does charge the school for the one copy. The senior class advisers have raised some questions. Does this violate any music rights or rights in the images? Secondly, this year the advisors would like to be able to give each senior a CD copy of the slide show at no charge. Do we need to check with the company who made the video to see if we have the right to give away copies?*

© What is your contract with the company? Has the company cleared the rights to the music? Just putting the music on the CD as accompaniment requires a synch license, plus duplication rights if you are making copies. You will need to pay those rights for all the copies you are going to make. And you are correct about the images on the CD. You probably need clearance for both the video and the recognizable images of individuals. Plus, inquire into the source of the images/video used in the CD. The person who created the image/video owns the rights to the work. The video company cannot appropriate those images without the permission of the copyright holders.

? *Does the Family Movie Act of 2005 provide protection for companies that edit movies then sell them? I know it allows families to do so in their homes. I am now hearing that this act does allow companies to resell edited movies and that these edited movies can be purchased by schools and shown in schools without copyright infringement. I am confused. Can you please help me better understand this piece of legislation so I am providing correct information to my teachers and parents?*

© The Family Movie Act of 2005 allows companies (only one company—ClearPlay—is currently doing this) to encode certain movies so that they will skip objectionable parts when played on specifically designed players. ClearPlay technology doesn't edit the movies; it uses invisible coding files that combine with the DVD to mute or blank certain types of objectionable content. This congressional permission has been allowed only for home use (the repeated specific inclusion of the word *family* is your clue there). Movies created by Clean Flicks and the other companies that made copies of works to expurgate offensive content are doing so without the permission of the copyright holders. The companies were sued by a group of directors and movie studios, and they were found to be infringing copyright in mid-2006. They have been enjoined from editing movies. Note that in a copyright fair use analysis of video use under section 110(1), one of the requirements is that a school showing be made from a legally acquired copy of a video. The videos that Clean Flicks et al. sold were infringing, so they are not legal copies. They should not be used in schools.

? *Our technology coordinator is purchasing a DVD burner in order to make copies of classroom/library videos. She says we are not violating copyright because we are making archival copies, even though we would now be using the DVD version rather than the VHS version. Is this correct?*

Your technology coordinator is right about one thing: she is making an archival copy. The problem is that archival copies of video are not permitted under current U.S. law. The only medium given automatic permission for archival (backup) copies is computer software. In fact, video producers routinely sell archival rights. The technology coordinator would also be changing the format of the materials, and the reason she is changing the format is to avoid purchasing the program in the new medium (DVD). While a transfer might be justified if the materials weren't available in digital format, any time you can purchase a DVD and yet you convert that work from another format, you should hear all sorts of alarm bells going off.

? *I know that Clean Flicks and similar companies are pro-hibited from selling expurgated copies of movies, but there are several companies in Canada selling "family friendly" films. Are those legal?*

© I don't purport to know Canadian copyright law, but it is fairly close to U.S. law on fair use (fair dealing, in Canada) issues. Since Clean Flicks and several other companies lost their federal lawsuit in 2006, making and selling unauthorized expurgated copies has been illegal in the US. Perhaps the companies just moved to Canada to get around the U.S. ruling, but the copies would not meet the U.S. educational fair use requirements because the section 110(1) requirements demand a "legally acquired" copy. An infringing copy (these are infringing per the U.S. federal court ruling) is not "legally acquired," so you would not be able to use it under the fair use exemption.

? *Is there a way to tell after the shrink-wrap has been removed that the video is licensed for public performance or has other restrictions?*

© No, there generally isn't, but it may have a license document inside or some licensing information at the beginning of the tape. I haven't personally bought one of those, though I have seen them. It's rather like computer software. There isn't any physical difference between software that comes with a three-user license, meaning you can install it on three computers, and software that has a one-user license. If you are challenged, the burden of proof is on you to prove you have the necessary rights. You would want to have documentation of where you bought something, obviously. I recommend that a school always have documentation of where/when licensed materials were purchased and what license was available at that time. That information can be kept in the 540 MARC field.

Go to my Web page at www.carolsimpson.com/public_performance_rights.htm for a list of companies that generally provide public performance rights (PPRs). You will note that some of those only provide PPRs when materials are bought from a specific supplier. In those cases, you want to be absolutely clear that you have proof of the source of the video.

? *Is it legal for a school library to use a DVD player that has the ClearPlay software loaded on it to filter out language, violence, etc. from a DVD disc? I do know that it is not legal to use edited DVDs purchased from companies that edit them. But it seems, from what I have read, that it is legal to use the ClearPlay software.*

© ClearPlay software was officially cleared by the United States Congress via the Family Movie Act. However, the act only specifies home use; therefore, it is an open question whether use in a school would be permitted.

? *I need information on the legitimacy of transferring VHS tapes to DVD format. These tapes were copyrighted in the 1980s by a company no longer in existence. The videotapes are no longer available, much less in DVD format. We are swiftly moving to providing classroom teachers with a PC that has a DVD component, but no VHS capability. What can I legally do with those VHS tapes that are no longer available for purchase?*

© At this moment, you are pretty much stuck. Changing from analog (VHS) to digital (DVD) is creating a derivative work. These films are undoubtedly still protected by copyright, so making the switch to DVD is at the option of the copyright holder. This format transfer is not generally a fair use (you are copying all of it, it is a creative work, and you are affecting the copyright owner's potential market for his own DVD version), and it certainly isn't a statutory right. There is not even a statutory right to make archival (backup) copies of video—that right exists only for computer software. You must consider that the owners of these programs may have actively chosen NOT to go to DVD because the films are out of date, and they don't want them "out there" in the same way that you may withdraw from the market a set of perfectly good encyclopedias because they are out of date. They don't want their names associated with something inaccurate or untimely.

In addition, you apparently cannot claim the exemption for copying works that are damaged or deteriorating, lost or stolen. You explained that the reason for the transfer was for convenience—the rest of your collection is moving toward DVD, so you want these to be in DVD as well.

Your one true option is to contact the copyright owners. While the publication/distribution company may be out of business, their assets have gone to someone, and that includes the intellectual property of the company. You could try to track down the producers, writers, or narrators to see if they know (they should be getting residual checks from the company), because one of them will frequently recapture the intellectual property if the company doesn't exploit the copyright. You can also do a search at the Copyright Office to see who the current owner of the copyright is. That is not always a successful search, but new owners of intellectual property are supposed to register their ownership, and it may be recorded there.

Under DMCA [Digital Millennium Copyright Act], there is an option for *libraries* to create digital archival copies of media that are "obsolete" when an unused replacement is not available to purchase, but VHS doesn't yet qualify for that category because you can still buy VHS players. Once those are totally off the market, you will be able to make backup copies, but there is still a down side—you can't distribute the archival copies outside of the archiving library.

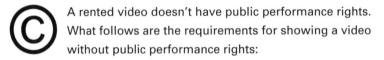

? *Our broadcasting system is up and running here at my school, and teachers have been told that they cannot broadcast videos rented from any video store. They were also told no broadcasting of videos individual teachers have purchased for their own home use. That doesn't sound right.*

© A rented video doesn't have public performance rights. What follows are the requirements for showing a video without public performance rights:

1. Must be a nonprofit educational institution

2. Must be shown by teachers and students in a regularly scheduled class

3. Must be shown in a classroom or other instructional place

4. Must be shown from a legally acquired copy of the program (the rental store bought it, so it is legal)

5. Must be a material part of *direct* instruction

Now, before we go on, we need to address the issue of "broadcasting." I assume that this is a media distribution system, not true broadcast. A media distribution system does not leave your campus. If you are sending this programming off campus, all educational exemptions are out the window and you must purchase broadcast rights, which are very expensive. If the distribution stays within your own campus, you can rely on the regular educational exemptions.

You may use a "home use only" video from ANY legal source as long as you meet the five aforementioned exemptions. ("Home use only" translates into "no public performance rights.") If you don't (using a video for reward, for example), you need public performance rights. Of course, all discussion of school use of "home use only" video is moot if the purchaser has agreed to some license or terms and conditions that limits where the video may be played. In that case, the license controls.

? *I know you can make backup copies of software for yourself. But what about DVDs? If you buy a DVD you can play it on your TV, portable DVD player, or laptop/desktop computer. What about downloading it to a handheld PC?*

© DVDs are not computer software. The archival provision is for computer software. DVDs are video. The Audio Home Recording Act allows you to change format for personal use of audio (records to cassettes, for example, or CD to MP3 player). There is not, however, a similar exemption for video. Also remember that the ability to make backup copies of computer software includes the requirement that you don't *use* the backups unless the original is unusable.

If you purchase the video and wish to play it on your handheld PC and the PC does not require conversion to another format, you could use the PC to play it. But the copyright owner would argue that retaining the copy on the handheld PC would be an archival copy, not permitted unless you have permission. So play it on the PC, and erase it when you are finished. This recommendation would apply to your use at home. I would not make the same recommendation for use at school. Private, personal use has certain more relaxed analysis than use in a public situation by a governmental entity such as a school.

? *A teacher is looking for a clean video version of an award-winning entertainment movie to show to her class. She frequently checks www.cleanflicks.com to look for movies, but her preferred title is not listed.*

© Warning: Cleanflicks.com edited videos have been held by a federal court to infringe copyright law. Only expurgation using the ClearPlay technology has been found to *not* infringe copyright, and that applies only in a home setting, per federal law. You may not use an infringing video in a school setting without also infringing copyright law. One of the required section 110(1) five factors in exempt educational AV use is that the copy you use is a legally acquired copy. Cleanflicks edited videos are not legal. At the time of this writing, cleanflicks.com's website was labeled "under construction," so apparently the company is not actively selling videos. You might be able to locate a sanitized version of the film through Swank (www.swank.com), which provides authorized edited versions for airlines and cruise ships. If the copyright owner releases his own expurgated copy, that copy is certainly legal.

? *If Limewire, iTunes, and YouTube are legal sites and free, then is it illegal to download music from them? Can anyone download movies legally?*

© There are no simple answers to those questions. As in all legal issues, the answer is "it depends." First, Limewire was found guilty of illegal activities in sharing copyrighted content, so I would not characterize it as a "legal site." Yes, it is legal to download music from iTunes and others, if you pay for it (or the site offers it for free download under the authority of the copyright owner). Some music sites have free download music put up by the copyright holder. You get some sort of license with what you download, and you are bound by that license. With iTunes, you have personal rights, just like you do when you purchase a CD. You can give away your copy (unless the license says you can't), but you can't duplicate your copy beyond the limits of the license, nor can you publicly perform your copy unless your license grants you public performance rights. For downloaded movies and television series, your use also depends on the license you get with your download. You can be certain that if the downloaded movie is in theaters, will be in theaters soon, or was once in theaters and is not yet in the public domain, the download is probably illegal unless you get it from a reputable commercial site.

? *The library staff in a very affluent district has made VHS video copies of DVDs and DVD copies of VHS videotapes so teachers can have copies of whichever version they prefer! They even have stickers on each item saying "DVD (VHS) copy also available." Is this practice acceptable?*

© The Digital Millennium Copyright Act allows a library to make a format transfer when hardware to play the original format is no longer available in the marketplace. Under that definition, VHS isn't obsolete yet, so you can't make preservation copies of the VHS tapes. DVD is an even newer technology, so it is not obsolete yet, either. (And preservation copies can't circulate beyond the library walls anyway). They can also make a transfer if the copy they have is damaged or deteriorating, lost, or stolen and an unused replacement is not available in the marketplace. Those circumstances don't seem to apply to this situation, either. If you need some backup on your position, you can get a copy of the law online: th e Copyright Office website has Circular 1 in pdf for free download.

Generally | *PPR Extortion?*

? *We recently received the following from a popular cable television network that often shows programs suitable for classroom instruction after we inquired about getting MARC records for a program we purchased:*

There are many rights, restrictions, and licensing issues involved with showing a video in a public performance. Any classroom, meeting or training session is considered a public performance. Public performance rights are only available in the following ways:

1. *By purchasing the program directly from our network; or*
2. *By using the off-air recording rights for schools (taping certain preapproved shows and using them for one year from the airdate. This would be programming during [name and time of series1]; [name and time of series2]; [name and time of series3]. The videos that are available through our network are formatted and copyright-cleared for permanent use. These videos are specially designed and edited for classroom use. They also come with teacher guides.)*

The video in question is used in a "face to face" teaching situation and, I believe, falls under the section 110(1) statutory permissions. We had not asked about public performance rights, so we don't understand their response. Is this a new twist, or just a way to get licensing money from schools?

© The response was probably a boilerplate response. The program that you bought must have been shown on that network. Because it is a cable only network and the standard school off-air taping permissions do not apply (the 10/45-day limits), the network may place any restrictions it likes on its programs. This particular network *only* permits schools to tape [series1], [series2], and [series3]. Since your program was not on any of those series, recording off air isn't legal. However, if you purchased the video from the network directly, you can look to the information in the last half of the message. If you purchased the video from a jobber, however, the video has no public performance rights. You are correct that if you meet the five requirements of section 110(1) you do not need public performance rights for a classroom showing. Nevertheless, if you did not purchase the program but rather leased or licensed the program, you are stuck with whatever rights were issued with that license. Those rights may include not being able to use the program in a public performance, including a classroom. Always ask if you are purchasing your copy, or if you are licensing it. You can see more information on individual producers and the rights they offer by going to my website at www.carolsimpson.com and checking my Public Performance Rights page.

? *We have a Movie Licensing USA contract to cover class-room performance of videos. Teachers want to buy DVDs at a local megastore to use in class. Can we do that?*

© There are a couple of considerations here:

1. Is the video restricted? Some videos (and books) sold at Walmart and Sam's Club are shrink-wrapped with the wording "Not for use at libraries and schools." If that is the case, you may not be able to use the videos at school if your federal circuit court has ruled that shrink-wrap licenses are binding within your circuit. If it has, fair use doesn't apply here because you agreed to a license when you opened the video.

2. Is the producer of the video on your license with Movie Licensing? Your license with Movie Licensing doesn't cover *every* producer, only the ones in your license. If you are going to use a video from one of the licensed companies, any legal copy (including those bought at a discount retailer absent a shrink-wrap license) will work, even one that says "home use only."

? *My library owns a 1986 videotape that is deteriorating rapidly as it is used by our teachers every year. We have searched everywhere we can think of to find a replacement to no avail. The foundation that produced the video no longer exists. Is it legal for us to make a DVD copy of this tape so that our teachers may continue to use the content? What guidelines govern duplicating out-of-print video?*

© The section 108 rule on library archival copies would let you make a digital copy (up to three copies, actually) of a deteriorating work, but the copies cannot leave the library. You would be able to circulate a VHS copy of the deteriorating video.

? *I need to find information on video duplication. Our school nurse wishes to make copies of three videos on health issues, which she needs to show at all five schools in the district. Of course, the videos are copyrighted and warn of federal laws in that regard. Can she make the copies for these showings?*

© Making copies of copyright-protected videos is a right that is reserved to the copyright owner. Without explicit permission, one cannot make additional or backup copies of an undamaged video presently available in the marketplace because making the copies literally takes money out of the pocket of the copyright owner. The permissions given to schools are limited. The primary fair use exemption that a school gets for video is being able to *show* the video without paying additional public performance fees. The exemption doesn't mean that the school can avoid paying for the copies they use to make the showings, however. She can take the legally purchased copy of the video to all five schools and show it under the educational exemption. You might also be able to negotiate a fee with the copyright owner to duplicate your own copies at a lesser fee than purchasing an additional four copies.

? *Have you heard about DVD players with filters for objec-tionable language? Is it legal to filter? I thought not, but the vendor assures me that it is.*

© Yes, DVD players that use downloaded files to track a video and mute or blank the program at specific frames are legal by federal law. The most popular name for this technology is ClearPlay. In contrast to some of the outfits that sell censored DVDs, ClearPlay changes are ephemeral, so there is no derivative work and no illegal copy. It's a win for everyone. The downside is that you must pay a monthly subscription fee to have access to the files that match with your DVDs.

? *A senior English teacher is comparing a scene in* Hamlet *from three different filmed versions. The school owns all three versions of the* Hamlet *videos, and we also subscribe to a movie licensing service. The teacher would like to transfer those three scenes to a single recording so he doesn't have to keep switching out tapes in the player. Is this okay?*

© What you describe is called "making an anthology." Anthologies are not permitted in the print guidelines, which are the only copy guidelines we have other than backup copies for computer software. There is no specific writing in the law to say that anthologies are or are not permitted in video. But the off-air recordings guidelines from 1976 specifically say that one may not make anthologies of off-air excerpts. A Register of Copyrights rule allows anthologies of video clips, but only for higher education use by media studies professors. Your movie license has nothing to do with this use because it only gives you public performance rights, which you don't need anyway since this is a curricular showing and meets all of the AV guidelines (section 110(1) of the law). While you might not be caught if you created and retained such a recording, I wouldn't want to have this sort of thing hanging around. If the teacher plans to do this, I would say to use as little as possible and make the copy only for the time he will use it in class, then *erase*.

? *What do you know about companies that edit R-rated movies and then sell the edited version? The companies to which I have been referred are Cleanflicks.com, Editmymovies.com, and Familyflix.net.*

© Use caution with those companies. Several were targets of copyright infringement suits filed by the copyright owners of the edited films. The United States District Court in the District of Colorado (where the suit was filed) ruled that the copies the companies sold infringed the copyright of the various movie studios that owned the copyrights. None of the companies had permission to edit the films, and the copies they sold were illegal. Remember that one of the factors in doing a copyright fair use evaluation to use video is using a copy that is "legally acquired," so using one of the illegal copies could be risky. If you want an expurgated copy that is legal, the only company I know of is Swank. Go to (www.swank.com) and choose "other" from the options.

? *A teacher returned the videotape of* Oedipus Rex *that he just borrowed the day before. He hadn't used the tape yet; he just ran it through a digitizer and loaded it into his computer. He plans to project it through his computer and the projector. Isn't this a copyright violation?*

© Yes. He has made a copy and an adaptation, violating two rights of the copyright holder. Educational exemptions allow certain public performances, but making copies and adaptations are not part of those permitted fair uses. This use doesn't meet the general fair use guidelines, either, though such use *at home* is probably not going to get anyone in trouble as long as the copies are not distributed. At school, the rules on analog-to-digital transfers are that such transfers are only acceptable if a digital copy is not available in the marketplace and the format in which the tape exists is considered "obsolete." You didn't specify the format, but at the time of this writing only Beta format video and laserdisc are obsolete. As long as VHS players are available in the marketplace, the format is not considered obsolete for the purposes of this analysis.

? *Depending upon the production company, we have discovered that many videos do not fall under "fair use" even in the classroom (with the lesson plan, direct instruction, and with a legal copy of the video). We even defined what "fair use" was, and the company agreed that they understood, but that, although the other videos that we owned would not necessarily need a license for use in the classroom when used with a lesson plan, this company restricted the use of their videos in any setting other than personal use (at home).*

© The direct instruction piece (the five yes/no questions) is part of federal law. A company cannot just "decide" to not permit use of their materials under federal fair use exemptions. That being said, if the purchaser signs a license/contract or buys a copy with a shrink-wrap that says "not for use in schools and libraries," you are bound by that contract. In other words, you have fair use rights unless you choose to give them up through restrictive licensing.

? *We have many videos that are in foreign languages. Just because* Pinocchio, Beauty and the Beast, *etc. are in a foreign language, that doesn't make them exempt from fair use, does it? The foreign language teachers state that one of their standards is "immersing students in the foreign language by hearing the language." I have one teacher who brings in videos of* Friends *in Spanish. I need some solid clarification before I can take this to administration. I know it happens in our middle schools also. Thanks!*

© No, foreign language films still must be used under the statutory guidelines for audio-visuals. I used to teach French. Standard foreign language curriculum involves four skills: reading, writing, listening, and speaking. For the latter two, you have to have something to listen TO and speak *ABOUT*. As long as the film is being used with those objectives, the showing would certainly meet the AV fair use requirements of section 110.

? *Can staff show video in their classrooms that they have purchased from the iTunes store and now have on their iPods or laptops?*

© Barring some specific license for an individual video (which sometimes happens) or a general iTunes terms of service that prohibits using its videos in that manner, any legally acquired video may be used for direct instruction if you meet all the requirements of section 110(1) of copyright law. Section 110(1) is the five-factor assessment for exempt use of video for direct instruction.

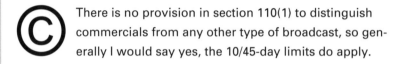

? *Some teachers use commercials taped from TV for a unit in their classrooms. Do TV commercials follow the 10/45-day fair use rule as taped broadcast TV? In other words, next year, they will need to find new commercials to use if they can't get permission to retain these?*

© There is no provision in section 110(1) to distinguish commercials from any other type of broadcast, so generally I would say yes, the 10/45-day limits do apply.

? *A teacher wants to show a movie for entertainment purposes on the school premises. He told the principal that he has acquired the performance rights to show the movie. He is going to charge students a two-dollar admission. Does the right to show a movie also include the right to charge admission and profit from it? The money would be used in some way for the students.*

© Public performance rights permit a showing to a group outside a family and its immediate circle of friends in situations that don't qualify for the educational exemption. However, they don't usually convey the right to charge admission. For the right to charge admission, an additional license or contract is required. There are brokers who will license or contract for-profit showings, also called nontheatrical showings. Note that "for profit" doesn't necessarily mean that you are going to make more money than you spend, only that you are going to collect admission fees.

? *The local theater has agreed to do a private showing of a video to students (50–100) who have earned the right by participating in a summer reading incentive program. The participating school must provide the video/DVD. Is it possible to become involved in this type of activity without violating copyright laws? If so, how?*

© I don't see how this type of showing could be within fair use. It's your video; you are just getting the theater for free. You will have students and teachers who are *not* part of a regularly scheduled class. You are showing the entire video. It isn't face-to-face instruction, and it isn't in a classroom or other instructional place, though the latter might be marginal. It doesn't meet *any* of the AV guidelines outlined in section 110(1) of the copyright act. Now, if this theater has some blanket license for the producer of the film you are planning to show (which you would want to verify), you might be okay. If the producer of the film is covered under a comprehensive performance license for the school, you may also be okay. Check your license to be sure.

? *I recently saw some DVDs at a great price in a local store. I didn't buy them because I wasn't sure about their licensing. Do the DVDs that I've purchased through vendors have public performance licensing and the ones in the bookstores just have home viewing? Is there a way to tell on the cover?*

© If you are getting public performance rights, you generally know it. A video bought at a consumer outlet is virtually assured to be home use only (but can be used instructionally because public performance rights are not required if the section 110(1) AV guidelines are met). Some videos purchased from some educational producers come with PPR when they are sold to schools directly (not necessarily through jobbers). See my Web page at www.carolsimpson.com/public_performance_rights.htm for a current list.

? *I use DVDs and videos for instruction only, so if I understand correctly, I can purchase them from anywhere for instructional use. If my PTA decided that they wanted to show one during recess, could they purchase a public performance license and show these same DVDs and videos?*

© Yes, no, and maybe. You can purchase them "from anywhere" for educational use *unless* they have a shrink-wrap license that says they are not for schools or libraries. I see those frequently at warehouse stores. If the PTA wants to show the videos at recess and the producer is covered by the any performance license the school has, you can show the videos for reward or entertainment purposes unless you have agreed through some license that you will not publicly perform the copy of the video. Remember, the movie licenses only cover about 20 of the most popular entertainment producers, such as Disney and Warner Bros. Verify first.

? *The fair use guidelines seem to be oriented to use of materials in a teaching situation. What about using a movie, or parts thereof, in a faculty meeting for the express purpose of discussing bullying on campus and ways to counteract it? We want to show clips of a movie on a cable channel. Should we try to get permission?*

© In such a situation, you fall back on the four tests of fair use. The section 110(1) educational exemptions apply only to face-to-face teaching, and these aren't students, they are employees. If you put the video into PowerPoint, however, you get the multimedia guidelines limits (three minutes or 10 percent, whichever is less) because you could make a decent case that this is a workshop. You might want to look at the Cable in the Classroom website (at www.ciconline.com) to see if the producer of that particular program has offered any specific permission for school/faculty use. That would speed up your evaluation of the copyright implications. Beyond the fair use and PowerPoint options, however, permission is your best route.

? Under the fair use guidelines and the fact that we have a performance license, when videos are shown in the classroom, must they be connected with a teaching activity? As a reward, can a class be shown a movie (remember . . . we have a license)?

© Keep in mind that a public performance license only covers entertainment films from a limited number of producers. It does not cover everything you might show. If you can meet the section 110(1) AV guidelines on that showing, you don't need public performance rights on that single showing. Each showing must be assessed separately. For reward showings, you may show the film only if the producer of the film to be shown is covered under your license. Reward showings of complete (or almost complete) films don't fall under the AV guidelines because they are not directly related to a teaching activity.

? *Can you use YouTube in the classroom? If curriculum writers find a video on YouTube that is scientifically correct and is appropriate for the high school classroom, could they use a YouTube video as part of the curriculum?*

© There are a lot of issues here to consider. The first is "Does the district have a policy on using YouTube?" That's not a copyright issue, but it may be controlling in this instance. There is much on YouTube that is inappropriate, so I would be surprised if your district filter let YouTube in.

On the copyright front, there are many videos on YouTube that aren't there legally. Episodes of *The Sopranos*, parts of movies and TV programs, and others are on YouTube. There are also videos posted without the permission of the a) creators and b) actors. Remember that everything relating to school fair use is predicated on a "legally acquired" copy of the work. If the work is not legal, you can't show it in school regardless of how good it is.

So assuming that everything is okay up to that point, how do you know if your use is fair? Go through the five yes/no questions for AV fair use. If you can pass that test, you should be good to go, as long as the YouTube terms of service do not preclude such use. However, I wouldn't build curriculum around any YouTube videos. They are fairly ephemeral.

? *In checking some videos I noticed this warning: "This videocassette contains copyrighted programs and is licensed for PRIVATE HOME USE ONLY. Public performance of any kind, including, but not limited to, school and library showings, is strictly prohibited." I have never seen a warning that specifically mentioned it could not be shown in a school setting. I guess we need to get rid of it, but before I do that, I was wondering if anyone else has seen this on videos in their collection.*

© If you are using a program for direct instruction (in other words, meeting the five tests of AV fair use), you don't need public performance rights. You are exempt from the PPR requirements in that instance. This is the "home use only" warning that is on so many videos. All it would appear to mean is that there are no public performance rights on that copy of the recording. But if you are doing *direct teaching* on that topic, and meet the other requirements of section 110(1), you don't need public performance rights.

In reading your question, however, it says that this video is "licensed." If this video was shrink-wrapped, or was purchased under some express or implied license, you may have waived your fair use rights by accepting the license. Without knowing from whom you purchased this video, and what purchase restrictions it had, it is impossible to be specific about what rights you may have purchased or to what limitations you may have agreed. Research the source and the producer for the most accurate information.

? *One of our elementary campuses shows rented or purchased movies routinely to large groups of students for after-school entertainment. In the past, the campus has purchased movie rights, but this year they do not want to spend the funds. What would have to be done for them to legally show either purchased or rented movies for entertainment?*

ⓒ To make these types of showings legal, you must have public performance rights. If you purchased PPR with the films (for purchased films), you can show them for any non-revenue purpose. If the film was *not* purchased with PPR (if you didn't pay much for the movie, if you taped it off-air, or if it has "home use only" on the medium or container, you probably don't have PPR) you can only use the tape for direct teaching situations.

You can't get PPR with rented videos under the default rental contract. You can arrange—either with the copyright owner directly, or with a licensing service—for PPR for a single showing. However, the rights are fairly expensive (about $125 for a typical Disney movie). Any legal copy (including rental, unless the licensing contract says the copy must be purchased) will work for those showings.

The most cost-effective means of entertainment showings is the site license from one of the licensing companies. At around $400 for an elementary school (depending on school size), that would cover only about four showings if licensed separately. The disadvantage is that it only covers the 20 or so major producers of entertainment videos. You generally don't need PPR for entertainment showings from most educational producers. You can find a list of educational video producers who offer PPR with purchase of their materials at www.carolsimpson.com/public_performance_rights.htm.

? *We would like to increase accessibility to resources by letting students use videos/DVDs in the library. All of our videos were bought as curriculum support. Some were bought by departments. They are usually played through a video distribution system. What are the copyright ramifications of the following situations?*

Scenario 1: Student missed class and needs to see a video that was shown.
Scenario 2: Student is interested in astronomy and we have a DVD on that.
Scenario 3: Student just wants to watch a video.

The public library can check out videos to patrons for home use. Are the possible snags that we are not "home" and fair use is not met because it is not face-to-face instruction?

© The first two scenarios should be okay as long as the showing is private to that student and not open to just anyone strolling by. Note, however, that the *Redd Horne* decision makes it problematic for students to view videos in the library just for the sake of viewing a video. *Redd Horne* held that private viewing rooms in a video rental store were public places when deciding if showing a video there was a public performance. Your public library probably does not allow video viewing in the library for just that reason. However, you can check out videos to students to take home with no problems unless you have some license agreement on those videos (check carefully in your ordering materials and in any stipulations that came with the shipments of the videos, as the licensing may be included there, and failure to object constitutes acceptance). You may have agreed in the license not to circulate your videos, or only to use them in direct teach situations.

? *Students in a business class as part of their curriculum set up a "business" that makes money. One particular group would like to get a DVD from the movie store and have a day at the movies. They would charge admission for the movie as part of their business plan. While the showing is tied to their curriculum, I'd like to clarify that piece. I think they need to contact someone for permission to use the DVD in this manner. If they need to ask permission, where would they go to do this? If they need to order a DVD on a temporary basis, where would they get it?*

Ⓒ If the students were just showing the movie on a topic of business organization to the members of the class, that use would qualify for fair use as direct teaching. But for the audience of this proposed showing, it isn't direct teach. When you do a movie analysis, think about the audience of the showing. If they are learning the topic being shown, you have at least the beginning of an educational fair use analysis (depending on the other four factors). If the audience is being entertained, your educational fair use argument fails. The students can get a copy to show for an admission charge from several sources, such as Swank (www.swank.com; choose "other" from the main menu) or other distributors. Some movie theaters will arrange the showing, and they take care of the licensing for you.

Chapter Six

Computer Software
and Multimedia

? *About four years ago, my school system purchased a basal reader that had Accelerated Reader tests for each story. The AR disk was lost or misplaced for the fourth-grade book. I cannot purchase a replacement copy. If I borrow this disk from another school in our district, would I be violating copyright laws?*

© If you purchased the original fourth-grade disk and didn't make a backup copy of it (shame on you for missing that opportunity—make one of the others ASAP), you can get a copy from another school and make two copies— one to use and one to put away "just in case." If you could purchase a copy at a reasonable price, you would be obligated to do so rather than making a copy from someone else.

? *We create and publish many manuals in our department for the various technology applications we use. A key component of these manuals is the screenshots we take of the menus and screen views in the applications we use. Is this in any way a violation of copyright?*

© It's a difficult question to answer. There are not any commercial cases on screenshots such as you describe. In fact, a Westlaw search of the term "screenshot" brings up only two cases, neither of which have applicability here. If you go to the websites of the software manufacturers, you often-times find permissions for screenshots for reviews, manuals, etc. Microsoft gives a blanket permission as long as the person using the shots is not saying anything disparaging about the product (!). On one hand, you can make a good case that this is minimal use and likely fair use (you are nonprofit, the amount used is small, and it is published, but it is creative), but the software manufacturer could make a case that the "look and feel" is the essence of the work.

All in all, since your use is fairly limited, if you are certain to keep the manuals within the district (include a notice that use is restricted to the district) and you cite the source of the screenshots ("all screenshots in this manual are taken from Microsoft Power-Point"), you should be safe.

? *Our sixth grade asked if it was okay to put a piece of paper up to a computer screen and trace a drawing (this would be for a student to do). The teacher wondered if he was able to legally do that, as well.*

© A tracing would be a copy, just as a freehand copy would be. The method of reproduction is not terribly important to an analysis. Copies do not have to be exact to be considered copies. The method of making the copy isn't very important. But just because something is a copy does not make the copy an infringement. Therefore, your students may trace the computer screen and use the single copy for personal use or their own education without many copyright problems. Your teacher, on the other hand, needs to consider how many copies he plans to make of the tracing and for what purpose he will use the copies. Take a look at the print guidelines for the rules on single and multiple copies for teachers for the rules based on what his planned uses are.

? *A teacher is making a PowerPoint presentation for a group of teachers and students. He wants to insert clips from movies. I thought this was a change of format and not allowed, but it is educational and the clips are short. Does the change in format override the fair use? Could he show the clips directly from a DVD (one at a time) if they are not embedded in the presentation?*

© Check the multimedia guidelines for the rules regarding using video in a presentation (see www.washington. edu/classroom/emc/fairuse.html). Provided he meets the use conditions outlined in the guidelines, he can use up to three minutes or 10 percent (whichever is less) of a movie in a Power-Point presentation. And as always, if the multimedia guidelines don't allow enough of the video, he can always fall back on a standard fair use assessment.

? *If I download 10 percent, or 30 seconds, of an audio to insert into Movie Maker, can I use that same 30 seconds as a loop, repeatedly throughout the project?*

© Under the multimedia guidelines, you can use 30 seconds of audio (or 10 percent, whichever is less) in a multimedia presentation. The source of the audio must be a legal one, so use caution when downloading. The guidelines do not say how many times you can use the clip in a given presentation, so I would argue that a loop is not prohibited.

? *We made a video for a centennial celebration. All the work in the video was created by the children except for some images (sources of images are documented with each image) and short music clips (in accordance with fair use guidelines). Parents who saw the video at the program want copies of it. Do you think this can be legally copied?*

© Each child who worked on the video can have a single copy per the multimedia guidelines. Remember that a multimedia project must have a statement that it may not be copied, along with a mediagraphy citing the source of any copyright-protected material used within.

? *I have a student who is preparing a multimedia presentation for a History Day competition. He wants to use copyrighted music, and I've advised him of the 30-second guideline. My question is, even if he stays within the time limit, does the fact that his presentation will be in a public forum to be judged put him outside the parameters of fair use for educational multimedia?*

© The multimedia guidelines specify where projects incorporating copyrighted content may be used. In class is a given. It also says that the student may retain and use such presentations as long as the use is "personal." Of course, "personal" isn't defined. The student could probably make a case that this use is personal. Nevertheless, if he should win, he can't give permission for the winning presentation to go up on the Web or be distributed on a CD-ROM or other vehicle because that is beyond "personal" use. He would need to justify each copyrighted element under a fair use assessment.

? *A teacher has students create commercials using music that has been downloaded from the Internet. He wants to know if it is legal to use the music in their commercials. I told him that it wouldn't be if it had been downloaded from a pirate site. Using your book, I was also able to tell him about the 30-second limit under the multimedia guidelines and that he wouldn't be able to show it on our local cable station (because students in the class are the only ones allowed to view the copyrighted material). Did I advise him correctly?*

Ⓒ Under the multimedia guidelines, 30 seconds is the recommended (approximate) limit for music that is more than 300 seconds long. For works less than 300 seconds (five minutes), the guidelines recommend using only 10 percent. The guidelines state that the student's use must be only for class or personal use (showing it to Grandma, for college applications, etc.), so cable distribution would probably not be a good plan. The entire use is predicated on a legally acquired copy of the work being used. If the student and teacher are sure the site is pirated, it would be a bad thing to use anything from the site (and a horrible example to set). But if they pay for the music (like through iTunes), the copy would be legal and would be okay. Remember that the guidelines are just that—guidelines. We know that the limits in the guidelines are safe, but if you need a little more than the guidelines, you can always fall back on a standard four-factor balancing fair use assessment under section 107.

? *In the October 2009 issue of Library Media Connection, you answered a copyright question about a teacher who has created commercials using music downloaded from the Internet (possibly pirated). You advised that if the teacher purchased the music legally, such as through iTunes, the copy would be legal and would be okay. I'm curious what you meant by okay. Does this mean the school could use the entire song in the multimedia production rather than following the 10 percent rule? The iTunes song license does not give a clear answer to these questions.*

© No, the same rules apply to iTunes music as would apply to a CD. I just meant that an iTunes copy is "legally acquired"—one of the requirements to use the music under the multimedia guidelines. The same rules would apply about where and how much to use.

Chapter Seven

Internet and
Distance Learning

? *I am creating an educational resource website that compiles resources and groups them into related topics on different Web pages (off of the main index page). I give credit for the resource (i.e., I do not claim to have created the resources). I only "link" to resources, not download or cut-and-paste into my site or put them in a "frame." My understanding is that it is okay to "link" to resources. However, now I'm reading that "deep" links may not be okay, could be a copyright conflict, and may require permission from the author. Is this true? To only link to the "homepage" would defeat the purpose of compiling resources that are designed to save time and provide ease of use in obtaining information on related topics. The reader would need to "hunt" through the pages to find the information I am referring to, which would not serve any useful purpose. Is it okay to provide these deep links without written permission from the site's owner?*

© As a general rule, it is okay to link to a website. That being said, we are talking about the homepage of a website, the main page that the site designer/owner has determined is what they want you to see first. For commercial websites, that viewing experience is set up with a lot of care and control. There may be information about their products, announcements, and advertisements with sponsors/partners that are predicated on a visitor viewing a site in a specific manner.

There have been a few lawsuits about deep linking, such as the Microsoft/Ticketmaster case. The reasons for these suits are those I previously stated. The site owner/creator may feel that the person linking is misrepresenting the site/information by just using a small portion and that misrepresentation would impair the value of his site. The owner of the Dilbert comic strip has routinely demanded that those linking to the Dilbert cartoon of the day break deep links and framed links to that page. The site owner has the prerogative to determine how someone can access/view the site by setting terms of service or linking policies. This doesn't necessarily say that the site owner would win in a lawsuit, but it does mean that he could file a suit that wouldn't get tossed out of court at first blush, and the site owner could make your life quite miserable for a long time.

? *Is it legal for me to post thumbnails of books I am highlighting on my Web page? Do I need permission from each individual publisher?*

© There is no clear answer to this question. Attorney Mary Minow, writing on the Stanford Fair Use website, says that the question is not clear cut by any means (see blog.librarylaw.com/library-law/2008/08/book-jackets--.html). The book covers are copyrighted images, either as part of the book itself, or possibly copyrighted by the artist and used by the publisher under some license. Publishers receive revenue from licensing images through vendors and book jobbers (usually for catalog images, but Web use can also be negotiated), so they are less likely to give gratis permission. There are the standard fair uses such as criticism, but that would have to be criticism of the *cover*, not necessarily of the work within.

For things such as your state's book award nominees, the sponsoring organization frequently gets permission for participating libraries to use lo-res images in bookmarks and other promotional materials. You could inquire there for that sort of use. I would also inquire of specific publishers. Many publishers have banks of images that they allow press to use for reviews and such, and those may be available for your use as well. You just need to know the secret location of the images. You might be able to get some of the big K–12 publishers to give blanket permission for use of their jacket images. Since the vast majority of the books in your library come from a small segment of the publishing world, with a few well-placed emails you could get permission for almost everything in your catalog.

What are the chances of you getting caught? Well, on an open Web page, they may be higher than you imagine. Playboy Enterprises developed Web search robots to scour personal Web pages for images from *Playboy*, and Playboy routinely sends out cease and desist letters to those identified with infringing images. Publishers are more and more protective of their images. I would certainly try for email permission first. If that doesn't work, a SHORT use (maybe a week) in lo-res would be much more defensible than more permanent use.

Also remember that some of the images on book covers (*Cat in the Hat*, for example) are trademarks as well as copyright protected. Any implied endorsement or affiliation would be actionable under trademark law as well as copyright, and since an entity will lose its trademark if allowed to become "generic," they are much more likely to prosecute on trademark grounds than copyright ones.

? *Teachers want to have students collaborate on a publicly accessible wiki on a given topic. The thought is that students can cite sources the same way they would for a paper. They would also link to the quoted or paraphrased material if it is already online. However, I noticed that one of our databases restricts re-using content without permission, but would this be educational fair use (scholarship and criticism)?*

© Remember that through license you can give up some of your standard fair use rights. Your database license may have done just that. You need to have your district's legal counsel review the license language and see if that is what has indeed happened. Also, remember that citation has little to do with fair use. While citation is an academic ethics concept, it is not necessarily required for fair use. Even items from the public domain should be cited.

How do copyright laws apply to translation of materials? We have a growing number of Spanish-speaking students and families, and we translate all of the documents we create. What are the rules for translating a copyrighted document such as a pdf file on the Internet?

A translation is a derivative work, and the right to create translations is a right owned by the copyright owner. Many copyright owners vigorously guard that right because they don't want just anyone making a translation that might be inaccurate or less literary than the original work. While there are laws that allow works to be converted into formats accessible to the print disabled, there are not similar laws regarding other languages. Obviously, your district has the right to translate any of its own documents. For other documents you may find online, your best bet is to ask permission, but don't be surprised if you are turned down, especially if the work is a creative work. On the other hand, the copyright owner of useful documents that could be of use to English Language Learners may be more than willing to allow you to translate the documents if you give them the translated documents to mount alongside their present English language versions. A fast phone call or email can answer that question. Perhaps rather than translating documents yourself, you might just make available a link to a Web application such as Babelfish that can translate documents on the fly.

? *As our district moves along with our student-produced book trailers, we are doing proper mediagraphy and attribution pages along with the fair use wording on the first slide of all of our trailers. If we are using images only from Creative Commons and music from freeplaymusic.com, can our trailers stay up on our school page for an indefinite amount of time, or is there a time limit?*

© Book trailers are multimedia projects according to the definition of the Fair Use Guidelines for Educational Multimedia. Look at the type of Creative Commons license you have for each image. There are multiple licenses that you can get from Creative Commons; some will allow you to do anything if you only attribute the source. Others say you cannot redistribute or modify the image. So, that is your first task. Look at the license with freeplaymusic.com as well. It may allow you to use the music in school but may not allow you to put it up on an open Web page. If you put the trailers up on a limited access page, your use could be evaluated under the TEACH Act or the multimedia guidelines. Neither of those will allow you to leave the trailers up indefinitely.

? *I posted both a link to a page and the content of that page (a poem) to an email distribution list for teachers. Someone objected because the content of the page was protected by copyright. I assumed that by giving the link where the poem was already published to the world, my posting was okay. Was I right?*

© In an academic paper, using an excerpt and giving attribution is fine. In your posting to the email list, you didn't give the authors or publisher, just the link and the text of the poem. Any time you reproduce the entirety of anything, you need to do a more thorough copyright analysis, including where you are sending it—this time to several thousand people around the world. A court would consider that to be making several thousand copies of it, potentially affecting the "value" of the work (which is for each viewer to see the advertisements or other information on the page from which you copied the work). So on a standard fair use analysis, your use was not for education (the recipients were not students), and you were not criticizing or commenting on the poem—you were merely reprinting it. Further, the work was creative. The law is not clear that posting something on the Web is "published," though it might be. Therefore, only one of the four fair use factors may come down in your favor. By just posting the link, folks could still see the work while giving the value (seeing the ads or other information) to the copyright owner—a win-win for everyone. So in short, posting the URL probably was fair; posting the entire poem probably was not.

As a suggestion for future use, you might post the first three to four lines of the poem, include some commentary, and then a link to where the reader could find the complete poem. Your limited use, coupled with the commentary, would likely be considered fair, and any interested readers could follow up with the link if they wished to read the rest of the poem.

? *I have a question about using clip art and children's books in schools for teaching purposes. For example, I bought a copy of Brown Bear by Bill Martin at a local bookstore. In this story, there is a brown bear, red bird, yellow duck, and other characters. I paid to join a clip art website and found clip art of a bear that's brown, a bird that's red, a duck that's yellow, etc. I use these pieces of clip art for a "brown bear game" where I read the story and the children put up the pieces of clip art on a pocket chart. Is this an okay use of clip art?*

© Assuming there is no restriction that you agreed to with your subscription to the clip art website, you can make a single copy of a print work (including a graphic) for your use in teaching. Your use appears to fall within that exemption.

? *A teacher asked if she could put the worksheet that goes with her Spanish textbook on her website when she puts lessons on the website. I told her I assumed the answer would be no—but that the company would probably give permission if she asked. Was I right?*

© I seriously doubt they would give permission. Remember, not only are you copying a consumable (something that is barred by the print guidelines), but you are also digitizing it and distributing (and displaying) it to the world! She could be violating four of the six reserved rights in one swoop! Now, if her website is password protected, you *might* get a different result under the TEACH Act, but even TEACH is touchy about consumables. After all, selling copies to students year after year is how consumables publishers make their money. When you digitize the pages, and share them with the world, you are taking money right out of the pocket of the publishers. They tend to get understandably upset when they find out.

? *Can a teacher put worksheets online (for a limited time) for students who are absent? We have paid for the right to copy them. The website would be password-protected.*

© This is a TEACH Act question. Under certain restrictions, materials can be put online behind a password. The key here is that these are "consumables." The TEACH Act prohibits digitizing materials that are consumable. Another key is that you have a license to reproduce. You need to examine that license carefully, looking for conditions that allow *digital* reproduction or transmission. If the contract is silent on those issues, you should contact the producer from whom you got the license. Be explicit about what rights you wish to license.

? *Our band teacher purchased music to use with the band. The music comes with a CD of the song(s) being performed. Can he put the songs up on the Internet for students to access if he uses a password?*

© This is a TEACH Act question. If he is going to be using the song to teach students (direct instruction, not just enrichment or extra-curricular activities) and this is a one-time use (he isn't going to use this CD every semester from now on), this use would likely be okay. The fact that he is using the whole song may be a bit more problematic, but the limited term of use and the restricted access via password are points in his favor. TEACH recommends not using complete or long works, but this song wouldn't be long, so I think you are okay here. The longer he uses the song, the poorer his TEACH Act defense would be.

Chapter Eight

Management
of Copyright

? *In your book, you state that fair use is to "provide support to teachers in a classroom while presenting content to students." What applies to administrators who are presenting to each other at meetings, to teachers at faculty meetings, to the school board, and at conferences?*

© Unfortunately, Congress, in developing and adopting educational exemptions for copyright-protected materials, didn't consider staff development to be within the scope of most of the educational exemptions. Students are those who are enrolled in a "degree-granting" institution (they get a diploma at the end). In-service teachers, however, are employees, not students.

There is one notable exception to that general rule. Because educational exemptions are medium-specific, one medium does allow limited use of copyrighted materials to staff: multimedia (e.g., PowerPoint, video productions, etc). So, if you can meet the multimedia guideline limitations, you can use those limits in what the guidelines call "workshops."

Of course, one can always fall back on the four-factor "weighing" scenario of standard fair use, as well. Those are far less clear and more subjective, but they are available to anyone at anytime.

? *Several teachers showed Disney movies at their school and were turned in. The superintendent thinks that the teachers are liable and that the district does not need to purchase movie licensing. What documentation (cases) or website would you suggest that could help clarify the responsibilities of the district and any ramifications that might occur?*

© First, not every use of a Disney (or other) entertainment-type film is an infringement. But when such use is obviously outside a direct teaching situation, the likelihood that the showing is a non-exempt public performance rises substantially. The reality of lawsuits is that everyone will be sued, district and teacher, seeking the deepest pockets. If the teachers were doing these showings "within the scope of their employment" (and that is interpreted fairly broadly in most cases), the district can be held liable under the law of "agency"—the employee acts as the agent of the employer, so the employer is usually liable for things an employee does unless the employer can prove that the employee is on a "frolic." For a school district to prove that an employee was on a frolic, they would want to say that students weren't involved during a school day, or that an explicit district policy had been communicated to all employees in a way that there was no doubt that this type of behavior would not be tolerated. Of course, proving that in court will be very expensive. Licensing through one of the licensing agencies is much less expensive, so many districts choose to purchase the license as insurance against just what you are facing.

? *Is there a place one should report observed abuses of copyright? For example, if someone (a librarian) has copied copyrighted videotapes onto DVDs, discarded the videotapes, and circulated the copied DVDs, should that be reported to anyone?*

© There is no requirement to report observed violations of copyright. However, many people do so with the encouragement of some of the rights societies who offer bounties for reports of potential infringements. AIME [Association for Information Media and Equipment] is one organization that takes care of some video infringements, as do Swank (www.swank.com) and the Motion Picture Association of America (www.mpaa.org). Alternatively, some report directly to the copyright owner. Disney, for example, reportedly offers a $10,000 bounty for verified infringement reports. While producers may say such reports are confidential, the reality is that if a lawsuit ensues, the identity of the informer may have to be revealed.

? *If you know that a school district is in violation of copyright, where do you go from there?*

© I will assume you have already alerted the parties involved, have documented your efforts, etc. Do you wish to report the district? If so, what you could do differs by the type of medium involved. For music, you report to the Recording Industry Association of America (www.riaa.com); the American Society of Composers, Authors, and Publishers (www.ascap.com); Broadcast Music, Inc. (www.bmi.com); SESAC (www.sesac.org); or the National Music Publishers Association (www.nmpa.org). Those groups are rights organizations, and they have authority to take action on behalf of the copyright owners. For motion pictures, you could report to Movie Licensing USA (www.movlic.com) or to the Motion Picture Association of America (www.mpaa.org). For print materials, you could report to the Copyright Clearance Corp. (www.copyright.com) or to the respective publisher. For graphics, report to the copyright owner. For computer software, report to the Software and Information Industry Association (www.siia.org). The Association for Information Media and Equipment (www.aime.org) also does some copyright infringement brokering, as well. Some individual copyright owners, such as the Walt Disney Company, also accept and act upon copyright infringement reports on their own. Some of the previously mentioned organizations and companies offer bounties/rewards for verifiable reports. Reports are only taken seriously if they include enough particular information that the organization can be certain that the report is accurate. Understand that you may be identified, directly or indirectly, in any resulting legal action. You should consult with an attorney before taking any action that might ultimately result in an unfavorable employment decision.

? *If we were to use short bits of music from CDs we own in a daily announcement program, would we be required to cite resources and use a copyright disclaimer at the beginning, as we do in a multimedia project?*

Ⓒ Anytime you use anything that you didn't create, you have an ethical obligation to cite the source. How can you expect students to cite their sources if you aren't doing it? A copyright attorney once told me that if you don't cite your source, it is always a copyright violation, no matter how little you use it or where you use it. A video production is arguably a multimedia production within the definition in the multimedia guidelines; therefore, following the limitations and requirements of the guidelines is a reasonable practice.

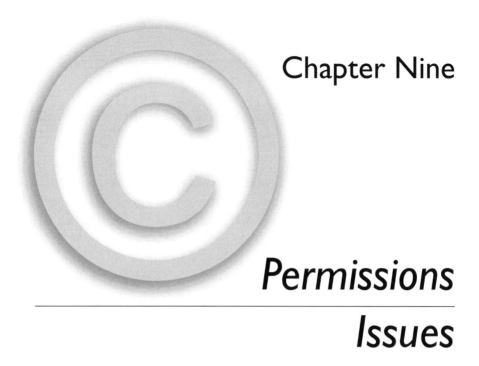

Chapter Nine

Permissions

Issues

Electronic Portfolio and Copyright Permissions

? *I have an electronic portfolio. Currently I have it on my personal website. I've emailed state legislators regarding pending bills for school and library funding. I've received both email and written letters from them. Would I need permission from the individuals to include the text of my email to the legislators and their replies in my portfolio?*

© You certainly would not need permission to post the emails you wrote yourself. You own the rights to those documents. As for the replies, a lot depends on who wrote the emails. Generally, emails are the intellectual property of the person who wrote them. The recipient owns the copy that he received but does not have the right to redistribute that copy. However, if a *federal* government employee within the scope of his duty wrote the email, there is no copyright, by law. Those emails you can distribute (via the Web or otherwise) as you wish. If state government employees sent the emails, you will need to check with your state to see if they claim copyright in the works of employees.

Characters for T-Shirts

? *A teacher is focusing on character traits and would like to use the characters from* The Wizard of Oz. *She wants to do a bulletin board and a T-shirt. She knows that she will need permission to do a T-shirt but does not know how to go about getting permission.*

© The original *Wizard of Oz* was printed around 1900, so it would be out of copyright protection. That is the ORIGINAL version. If you are using illustrations or adaptations done later than that, you would need to assess the copyright status of the respective items. If the teacher uses the illustrations from the original version of the book, all those are in the public domain, so she would be fine with the T-shirt.

Creative Commons

? *Are you familiar with the website of creativecommons.org? I recently attended a presentation where the presenter referred to this website as a means of using and "remixing" others' works with limited types of permission. Is such a thing as Creative Commons valid? Is it legal?*

© Yes, Creative Commons is very real, and certainly legal. The works licensed with Creative Commons licenses are (generally) protected by copyright, but liberally licensed. You need to thoroughly read the license for each item to know what restrictions (if any) apply to it. You can find Creative Commons licensed materials on many websites, such as Flickr, but they may be mixed in with works not so licensed. Always investigate the status of each individual work before using or distributing it.

New Lyrics in Performance

? *Our school is hosting a VIP luncheon. My principal wants to use the song "The Eye of the Tiger" from the movie Rocky. We have purchased a karaoke version of the song. My principal wants to change the lyrics to reflect our district's mission statement and goals. The adaptation of the song would not be recorded. It would be sung only by our school's choir for this event.*

I have requested copyright permission from the publisher of the karaoke DVD, the original artist, the company that currently owns the rights to the song, and Sony Music Entertainment, who owns the label on which the song was originally recorded. I have not received any responses back from these contacts.

This is my first attempt to try to get any type of copyright permission. My questions are: Do I need copyright permission to change the words for this type of school event? If not, can we sing our version of the song and cite the original publisher? Am I asking the right people? Other suggestions would be welcomed.

© Permission requests sometimes take quite a while. You need several forms of permission, assuming you didn't get permission to perform the music when you purchased the karaoke DVD. You need an arrangement license from the music publisher to change the lyrics. Performance licenses are available from ASCAP or BMI if you didn't get that with the karaoke DVD. You probably need a photocopy license to make copies of the sheet music for the performers. Photocopy permission is available from the music publisher. Because this is a one-time event with a very small audience, the music publisher might give you permission.

Index

Copyright Catechism II